LIVING YOUR *Magic*

LIVING YOUR *Magic*

How *to* Enjoy Your Mind
and Enjoy Your Life

LIFE IS LIKE A MAGIC TRICK. *Once you know how
the trick works, you can never be fooled by it again!*

DR. ROBERT ANTHONY

NEW YORK

LONDON • NASHVILLE • MELBOURNE • VANCOUVER

LIVING YOUR *Magic*

How *to* Enjoy Your Mind *and* Enjoy Your Life

LIFE IS LIKE A MAGIC TRICK. *Once you know how the trick works, you can never be fooled by it again!*

© 2020 DR. ROBERT ANTHONY

Published in New York, New York, by Morgan James Publishing. Morgan James is a trademark of Morgan James, LLC. www.MorganJamesPublishing.com

ISBN 978-1-64279-507-3 paperback
ISBN 978-1-64279-508-0 eBook
Library of Congress Control Number: 2019902200

Cover Design by:
Rachel Lopez
www.r2cdesign.com

Interior Design by:
Bonnie Bushman
The Whole Caboodle Graphic Design

In an effort to support local communities, raise awareness and funds, Morgan James Publishing donates a percentage of all book sales for the life of each book to Habitat for Humanity Peninsula and Greater Williamsburg.

Get involved today! Visit
www.MorganJamesBuilds.com

CONTENTS

INTRODUCTION

I've always been curious why some people change and why *most* people don't change when there are so many personal development trainings, seminars, books, and therapeutic interventions available today. With access to all these therapies, methodologies, systems, strategies, and techniques, we should be geniuses at changing our lives for the better—but we're not!

Another question I've asked myself is: "Why are we successful in some areas of our lives and in other areas we keep backsliding and can't seem to make the changes we desire?"

I used to think more information was the answer. If I could just understand myself, my psychology, and my past better, somewhere in there I would find the answer that would help me improve my life and I could help other people improve their lives as well.

The problem is that if we buy into the idea that if we keep studying and learning all these psychological and personal development methodologies, systems, strategies, and techniques, someday we will get "there"; it naturally causes us to keep looking for Wizards that can show us the way. In a sense, we're all "Off to See the Wizard!"

In the film, *The Wizard of Oz*, Dorothy (played by Judy Garland) gets caught up in a tornado and wakes up in the strange land of Oz. She's desperate to find her way home and goes on a quest to meet the Wizard whom she believes holds the key to her return. In the movie, when Dorothy and her friends finally meet the Wizard, he tells them that what they were looking for was not in Oz, but was inside of them the whole time.

There's a famous rock band from the '70's called America. One of my favorite songs on their album is "The Tin Man." There's a line in the song that acknowledges Oz couldn't provide the tin man with anything new since he already had what he needed.

The fact is, we already have everything we need to live our magic, but we either don't know it or don't believe it. And because we don't know it or don't believe it, like Dorothy, most of us spend a lot of time looking for Wizards who will give us the wisdom we need, the courage we need, and the heart we need to go on—but it's never about the Wizard.

There are many different kinds of Wizards out there. Some people think I'm a Wizard. (It's funny, because I do live in OZ—Australia), but what I've come to realize, like the Wizard of Oz, is that I can't give anything to anyone that they don't already have or don't already possess within themselves.

We tend to think that people who do the kind of work I do are Wizards because they seem to know more than we do. They write books, have degrees, certificates, training programs, and seminars and often make a lot of money as well, so they *must* know more than we do.

Well, here's the dirty little secret of the personal development business. None of those people, including myself, knows more than you do! What you're going to come to understand is that we all have this Inner Creative Genius within us that allows us to live a magical life. And if we trust it and learn how to get out of our own way, we don't need anything outside of ourselves to guide our lives or live our magic.

Let's Talk About Permission Slips

Before we start our journey together, I'd like to talk about the idea of "Permission Slips." Exactly what is a Permission Slip? Imagine giving yourself a slip of paper and on that slip of paper is written "I give myself permission to … (fill in the blank)." That is a Permission Slip.

So, what are we giving ourselves permission to do? We're giving ourselves permission to change so that we can have a different experience of life.

We can hand ourselves Permission Slips in various ways. This would include using crystals, astrology, meditating, following a particular religion or philosophy, using a personal development technique, reading a book, attending a workshop, hiring a coach, or going to a therapist.

Permission Slips are nothing more than you giving yourself permission to change in the way you prefer to change. They create a belief system within you that says when you do or practice the things on your permission slips they will allow you to have a different experience of life.

On the surface it may seem like they're necessary in order for you to have what you want and to be the person you choose to be, but, ultimately, you'll come to understand that those things are all the same. One is not better than another. Each permission slip will work because they're all doing the same thing: *you* giving *yourself* permission to have a different experience of life.

However, as you increase your understanding and gain more insight into your True Nature and how you create your reality moment-to-moment, you will arrive at a point where you will realize you actually don't need any of them. Instead, you can just say, "I don't need a Permission Slip other than giving myself permission to be who I am—to be myself."

"If I choose to use any type of personal development technique, meditation practice, therapeutic approach, or any teaching, philosophy, or religion and I believe it helps me to do what I choose to do and be, that's all well and good, but the truth is, I don't need any of them to change anything about myself or make myself a better person, because **I am that already**!"

Just knowing that will eliminate the need for most, if not all, of your permission slips, because you'll have access to the innate wisdom and deeper intelligence within yourself that will provide everything you need to change anything you desire and have a different experience of life.

And even in sharing this book with you, all I'm doing is giving you another Permission Slip. However, I like to see *Living Your Magic* as a way of giving you a Permission Slip to understand that you don't need a Permission Slip! So please keep that in mind as we go through our journey together.

Also, before we go any further, I want to make it clear that everything I'll be sharing with you is just my opinion. Sometimes people ask me, "Where is the evidence-based research and proof behind what you teach?" My answer is, "This is not an academic thesis". Rather than being academically led, my philosophy is to find what works, then use it and embrace it until you find something better.

What I'm sharing with you is what I've come to discover is true for me. I'm not going to tell you it's the "truth" and I don't expect you to blindly follow it or believe it. I've proven it for myself, but your job is to prove it for yourself.

If anything I say causes you resistance or you don't like it, please feel free to discard it. Take whatever resonates with you and apply it to your life and see if it makes a difference. There's nothing else you need to do.

THE RELATIONSHIP
BETWEEN "YOU"
AND "YOU"

L et's talk about the relationship between "You" and "You." The simple secret that will make your life magical and an explosion of synchronicity is to **know yourself** and to **accept yourself** for who you are.

One of the primary beliefs we have accepted about ourselves that was created by others is that we're psychologically and spiritually flawed in some way. The message we've received throughout our life is that in order for us to accept ourselves and be accepted by others, including God, there's something we need to believe, something we need to change, something we need to fix, something we need to acquire, or something we need to achieve. But what if all of that is just a story and if we give up the story, we can live a magical life? Let's explore this a little further.

The ultimate understanding that any one of us can have is the illusion of the made-up "Separate Self." Most of us are caught up in this illusion.

We believe this Illusory or made-up Self that we think we are is somehow real, but it's not. When we were born, this Illusory Self did not exist. We created this Self and gave it life and a separate reality though our thinking and our beliefs.

Your Illusory Self, also known as your Ego Self, is part of your subconscious programming. It's used as a reference point for living and giving you an opinion of what you're capable of, your limits, what you deserve, what's important to you, whether you think something's possible for you or not, etc. But here's what you need to know: this Illusory Self or Self-Created Identity is not who you really are. The mistake we all make is when we confuse our Illusory Self with who we really are—but who you really are is far more than you think you are.

When we came into our physical body it was necessary to splinter ourselves into two parts. One part is the *physical* aspect of ourselves and the other part is the *non-physical* aspect of ourselves. The physical aspect, or physical body, allows us to live here on earth and have a human experience. It also has a limited life span.

The *non-physical* aspect of ourselves is the part that lives in us and animates us and is sometimes referred to as our Essence, our Soul, our Spirit, or our Higher Self. I like to call it our Authentic Self. Throughout this book I will use them interchangeably. However, whatever you choose to call it, it's the part of us that has no limitation, no contamination, and is not bound by time and space.

Science often referrers to this non-physical aspect of ourselves as "Consciousness." In fact, this is the one place where science and spirituality actually agree with each other. And that is: we are Consciousness. We have awareness. Another way of saying this is that we are not a human who *has* consciousness; we *are* Consciousness having a human experience.

What this also means is that, at some point in our lives, when we're through with our Earth experience, we will leave our physical body behind and re-emerge back into the non-physical and continue to exist beyond this life as Consciousness.

Now, how do we know this? Because Consciousness or your sense of "Self" doesn't exist anywhere in your body or in your brain. Science cannot find it. You can have the entire right or left hemisphere of your brain removed and still have a sense of Self, so it's not in the brain. This leads us to the conclusion that Consciousness is infinite.

Most of us walk around thinking we're nothing more than a finite physical body with a brain because it's hard to grasp the idea that we are Consciousness—that we're **infinite**. If you understand that you are Consciousness having a human experience, then you also understand that everything happens *within* this infinite field of consciousness. Nothing can be separate from it.

So, what's behind all of this? I think it's safe to say that we're not in charge of the unfolding universe. What this means is there's an Intelligence or Center Point behind our existence that's common to all of us. Nothing exists outside of it, including you and me.

Different cultures and religions have different names they use to describe it. However, I'm not going to be pretentious enough to attempt to describe something that cannot be described. I think that any concept we have of the Formless Creative Intelligence behind life is not only made up but is too limiting.

From my perspective, if there is a Formless Creative Intelligence behind life that's spinning the planets, that determines the dominance and order in the animal kingdom, that controls the beating of the hearts of all who live, that allows our body to heal, that takes care of the changing of the seasons, that allows a seed planted in the ground to grow, then it's probably not my job to figure out what it is or how it all works. So, I prefer to use the term 'All That Is' and leave it at that. Everything that is created or will ever be created originates from this one Center Point or 'All That Is.'

We also know that everything in the known universe is comprised of vibrational energy. We're all made of the same energy. What we call matter is nothing more than energy in motion. It's just a question of how fast it is going that determines what form it takes.

Knowing that everything in the universe originates from this one Center Point and is comprised of vibrational energy, it's not difficult to come to the conclusion that each one of us is a unique, distinct **energetic vibrational signature** that is created from this Center Point. Each one of us has a core frequency or **signature vibration** that represents the non-physical aspect of ourselves.

Anything that is in alignment with that unique signature vibration is constantly trying to manifest through our physical self. If it doesn't manifest, it's because we are keeping it away with contrary beliefs and definitions that are out of alignment with who we are.

Living our magic is about of letting go of any beliefs or definitions that are out of alignment with that unique signature vibration, or who we are. Keep in mind, every belief you hold on to has a self-reinforcing frequency. So, whatever you believe to be true, whatever you believe to be possible, brings with it more of that same frequency and more of that same possibility. If you believe things are impossible or difficult then it brings more of that frequency and prevents you from knowing that something is, in fact, possible.

So, the primary difference between the Illusory Self that you call "you" and your non-physical Authentic Self is that your Illusory Self lives through your Ego, while your Authentic Self lives through All That Is because they're one and the same thing. They can never be separated. However, when you confuse your Illusory Self with your Authentic Self, that is when you run into all the problems and limitations you experience your life.

Now, let's just stop for a moment. As you're reading this you may be saying, "Hold on a moment. I just want to create a better life, I want to build a successful business. I want a happy relationship. I want to improve my finances, I want to get rid of the stress in my life, I am not interested in getting into religion."

It is important to understand that what we are referring to here is our Spiritual Nature that we're all born into that is *beyond* any religion. Religion is not the same as spirituality. Religion is what comes *after* spirituality. Every religion in existence is an interpretation of our Spiritual Nature. That's why there are so many religions. What we're talking about here is what comes *before* religion: your connection with this Deeper Intelligence behind life, your True Essence or your Authentic Self.

You might also be saying, "How could this possibly matter if I just want to build a successful business, improve my relationship, earn more money, find the right job or career, or get rid of the stress in my life? Why would it matter to me that beyond the experiences of my childhood, beyond the experiences of my body and what my body has been through, beyond my *memories of the past* and my *imaginings of future* that I have an existence in a non-physical realm that runs through me and through all of nature?"

It matters because you are a Creator. You are not only part of creation, but you're also that which creates. You create things with your mind, but you also have access to a Deeper Intelligence that is beyond your personal mind.

It's nice to know that if we align our personal mind and our intellect with this Deeper Intelligence, it tends to make our life so much easier and it allows us to create the things we desire without all the worry and struggle that we experience most of the time.

What we want to emphasize here is that our connection to this Deeper Intelligence is part of who we are. It's our True Nature. Our True Nature is like gravity. It will always be there, whether we believe in it or not. Gravity is a pre-existing force we're all born into. It works the same way for every person on the planet regardless of age, race, religion, gender, or sexual orientation. You don't have to believe in it or even remember it's there in order for it to work in your life. You will never float off the surface of the planet because you forgot about gravity. The always-present nature of gravity means you don't have to believe in it, or even give it a moment's thought.

We live in a reality where gravity keeps us safely on the ground. The same principle operates behind your True Nature. It also keeps you safely grounded. It allows you to live in a world of beautiful feelings, deep insights, and connection and communion with all of life.

What it also means to me is that as the boundaries between our True Nature and our Illusionary made-up Self dissolve, the boundaries between us and other people's True Nature and their Illusionary Self—whether it's an individual, group, country, religion, or culture—also dissolve.

From my perspective, if there was a way for people to massively transform their life, it wouldn't be about changing what they do or don't do, think or don't think, feel or don't feel. It would be about someone having an insight into their True Nature or their True Identity. What we're learning about is the existence of a deeper Self—a kind of a capital "S" Self that exists before the creation of our personalities and our ego.

Let's just step back a little so this makes more sense to you. When you were born, you were living directly from your Spirit or your Authentic Self. You didn't have an Ego or a personality. From that point on, your personal mind started to form not only an Illusory Self-Created Identity, but multiple personalities as well.

I'm sure you're familiar with something called the Multiple Personality Disorder. Most people who have this have suffered some type of trauma during their early years. When this happens, in order to survive, the individual invents "personalities" to deal with the abuse. The manifestation can be quite amazing. They can create different people who have different personalities and these personalities often have their own voices, facial expressions, etc.

Multiple Personality Disorder is among the most dramatic examples of how powerful we are at making things up in our head. However, keep in mind, we're all doing the same thing! As we go through life, we create multiple personalities, but we don't call it a "disorder." We change or alter our personality depending on who we're with and what situations we're in.

Most people form their personality in their early teens. Unfortunately, those are usually shaped from fear: fear of failure, fear of embarrassment, fear of loss, fear of not being good enough, fear of not having enough, and, as a teenager, the added fear of not "fitting in" or being accepted by our peer group. The result is that early in life we subconsciously create a false mask that we call our personality. This personality becomes part of our Self-Created Identity or how we see ourselves.

We then begin to think that we are this Self-Created Identity—the one that struggles with fear of failure, fear of embarrassment, fear of loss, fear of not being good enough, fear of not having enough, fear of lacking confidence, etc. So, in order to hide this from the world, we develop a kind of ego-based "mask" or personality designed to distract or misdirect the outside world. The goal is to keep people at enough of a distance so that they don't discover who and what we fear—and who we really think we are.

Our Self-Created Identity is the "Self" that most self-improvement, self-development, and therapeutic approaches aim to help us with. This is also the reason why our attempts to improve our self-image, self-esteem, and self-worth, don't work. They're about fixing, changing, or improving a made-up illusory "Self" that is not real.

At our core, our True Essence or our Authentic Self is solid and unchangeable. On the other hand, our Illusory Self is constantly changing. In Eastern teachings they talk about the "real" and the "illusory." Something that is illusory is anything that is temporary. It's anything that comes and goes. The fact that it comes and goes makes it "illusory." Anything that is "real" has permanence. It's eternal, immortal, and infinite. That's what we're pointing to when we talk about the Illusory Self and our Authentic Self. One is real and permanent and the other is made up and comes and goes.

You are not trapped in the Illusory Self-Created Identity that you call "you" because it's merely an accumulation of your thoughts about yourself. And in any moment, you can have a new thought about yourself. When you do, you are a different person. So, you are never stuck. Every moment is a new beginning. In any moment you can choose to live from your Illusory made-up Self, or you can choose to live from your Authentic Self.

So as we go through this experience together of *Living Your Magic*, you have to ask yourself this question: are you reading this or coming at this as an ego searching to be a better ego, an improved ego, a more self-developed ego, a more enlightened ego, or are you willing to put your ego aside and start connecting to your Authentic Self?

A metaphor for this is to see your life is an egg. The question is whether you are interested in decorating or changing the inside of your egg or are you beginning to see that you're inside the egg and hatching is a possibility. Hatching into freedom and hatching into your True Identity and *Living Your Magic*. The answer to this question will determine what you get out of this book, so consider it carefully!

Getting Stuck In "I Am"

Innocently, we create our Illusory Self through "I am" statements. Here are some "I am" statements. See if any of them resonate with you.

I am unworthy	I am a Christian	I am a victim
I am analytical	I am a Muslim	I am worried
I am beautiful	I am a Buddhist	I am afraid
I am ugly	I am a Catholic	I am depressed
I am thin	I am Jewish	I am confident
I am fat	I am a Hindu	I am unconfident
I am too short	I am a Democrat	I am sad
I am too tall	I am a Republican	I am bad
I am sexy	I am Labour	I am good

I am not sexy	I am Conservative	I am certain
I am clever	I am a Fundamentalist	I am stressed
I am stupid	I am gay	I am bored
I am a sinner	I am straight	I am lazy
I am rich	I am an alcoholic	I am anxious
I am poor	I am an addict	I am angry
I am unforgiveable	I am anorexic	I am upset

All of these "I am" statements, both positive and negative, are part of our Illusory Self or the ego. They're not who we are, but labels we put on ourselves.

There's nothing inherently "wrong" with "I am" statements—except when we forget they are all made up! Even the positive ones! However, the real danger is when our "I am" statements turn into "Identity" statements. In other words, when we can no longer separate who we think we are from our beliefs.

When someone uses an "I am" Identity statement, they can no longer separate what they believe from who they are. Anytime you turn an "I am" statement into an Identity statement you eliminate the possibility of using your critical thinking capacity and you shut off all objectivity.

From my experience it's very difficult to separate people from their Identity statements because if I challenge your beliefs, you will feel I've challenged your identity or how you see yourself because you cannot separate who you are from what you believe. Your knee-jerk reaction will be to resist anything or anyone who challenges your beliefs because you have attached your beliefs to your Identity. You can no longer separate the two. It's no longer a *label* you have put on yourself—it is who you are!

Keep in mind that any "I am" statements that are not in alignment with your True Identity or True Nature are made-up ideas you've accepted about yourself. You were not born with any of them.

When you were born you were not limited by any "I am" statement, but at some point, you came to the conclusion that they are true. And anytime you think something in your personal thinking is true you are going to suffer the limitation of that particular thought.

We're always going to have a made-up Illusory Self or an ego—and that's okay. That's the human bit. But as soon as we start *identifying* with it, as soon as it becomes our True Identity, we set ourselves up for suffering and limitation. However, when you are able to see your Ego Self for what it is, or at the very least you're conscious you're making it up, you are free to tap into the deeper wisdom of your Authentic Self and your True Nature.

If we're not buying into our illusory Ego Self or our personality, we can relax more and connect with our Authentic Self. When we let go of our made-up Ego Self, our True Authentic Self comes shining through. And because your Authentic Self has no judgment and no fear, you can thrive and live in a world of possibility instead of a world of limitation.

For me, the ultimate leverage point is when my Illusory Self (who I think I am) and my Authentic Self (who I know I am at my core) are in alignment. When they are, anything is possible for me. My life runs smoothly, and I am thriving.

But when there is a gap or disparity between the two and my Illusory Self or my Ego Self takes over, I am usually full of crap and so is my life! (Just so you know, "crap" is my code word for everything that gets in the way of living our magic.)

So, your ultimate leverage point is when your Illusory Self (who you think you are) matches your Authentic Self (who you really are). This is the point where you have the most power to thrive and live your magic. When I am in touch with that, anything is possible. Without it, very little is possible.

If you look at your life, you will see that you're either a Master of Possibility or a Master of Limitation. When I'm in touch with the wisdom of my Authentic Self, I am a Master of Possibility. Instead of fusing with my thoughts and thinking they are real and getting caught up in all my old ideas, beliefs, and contaminated thinking, I get fresh *new* ideas, *new* insights, and *new* solutions.

When I keep circulating my old ideas and beliefs in my head, or I keep thinking about my past or what is not possible, I become a Master of Limitation. When we are Masters of Limitation, we focus on our made-up Illusory Self or our Ego Self that is telling us: "That's the way I am" or "That's the way it is." When we do this, it creates a story about who we are and what we're capable of being and doing. Then we just keep adding more stories which confirms that original story.

Creating the life you desire and living your magic is not about replacing one story with another. It's about an understanding of how you can create a **new reality** moment-to-moment so that there's no story to live up to. If our life is about protecting our Illusory Self or our ego, we can't live anywhere near our full potential. Essentially, we're living from a tiny little fraction of who we really are.

This unique signature vibrational frequency that is our Authentic Self or our Spirit is also perfect! However, we are trained from childhood to look at our Ego Self and judge ourselves as imperfect, but that's all part of the brainwashing that society and those who want to control us try to make us believe. Whether it's religion, the government, or any other person, group, or organization, they're all invested in making us believe we're less than we are. If they did otherwise, they would all be out of business!

Because most people don't understand their True Nature, they often feel that they're less than they truly are. This causes them to focus on self-mastery or trying to become enlightened, but the purpose of life is not about trying to become enlightened or become anything else. It's about recognizing the Enlightened Being that *you already are—that you haven't accepted yet.* It's all there waiting to be uncovered if you will allow it to come to the surface.

So, the question is: which "Self" do we want to live from? The Illusory Self or Ego Self which is not real, or our Authentic Self which is real, eternal, and perfect? In any moment, we always have a choice.

Chapter 2

IT'S OKAY
TO BE HUMAN

There was a period in my life where I was on what some might call a "spiritual journey." I studied almost every major religion, including Christianity, Islam, Judaism, Hinduism, Mormonism, Buddhism, and almost every other type of "ism" there is out there. I also immersed myself in most of the New Thought and metaphysical teachings as well.

No matter how much I studied, searched, and participated in these teachings and religions I was constantly frustrated because there was always this gap between the spiritual nature I was seeking and the human nature I was living. This caused me to be judgmental or dismissive of my human nature. My human nature never seemed to catch up with my spiritual understanding.

What I later came to realize is that sometimes there is a time-lag for our intellectual understanding to catch up with our spiritual understanding before we can blend the two together. And if we get frustrated because they don't seem to line up, we go backwards instead of going forwards.

The other thing I was missing is that any time we search for something, we think we don't already have it. Put simply, you cannot find what you are searching for if you already have it. What I discovered was that I already had what I was searching for. When you realize you already have what you've been searching for, you step into a different world.

The way I have come to understand it is that our human nature and our spiritual nature are like a single coin. Our human nature is one side of the coin and our spiritual nature is the other side of the coin, but it's still just one coin! That's the *oneness* that these great spiritual leaders and teachers talk about, but we don't seem to "get it." I know I didn't!

Essentially what the original spiritual leaders and teachers were trying to teach us (before their teachings became convoluted by their followers) is that we are both human and spiritual—at the same time!

Earlier, we pointed to the fact that we are Consciousness having a human experience. Another way of saying this is we are a Spiritual Being having a human experience. We cannot separate the two. Our spiritual nature and our human nature are one.

I am sure you are familiar with what's often referred to as the Yin/Yang symbol. It is a symbol of opposites merging together. Most of the time it's displayed as a black and white circle divided in half by a wave. There's also a white dot in the black half and a black dot in the white half.

In this case, the white represents our spiritual nature and the black represents our human nature. They merge together as one. The white dot in our human nature and the black dot in our spiritual nature are there to remind us they are intertwined and not separated in any way.

When I look at this symbol it reminds me to stop splitting my human nature and my spiritual nature. As soon as we divide the two, the judgment comes in because one becomes "better" than the other, but by seeing them as one, the self-judgment automatically falls away.

What I love about honouring our human nature is if I understand that my humanness or my human nature and my spiritual nature are one, then if I put down or disrespect my human nature with all its mistakes, or what religion likes to call "sins," in a sense I am disrespecting All That Is because my human nature and my spiritual nature are one and the same!

The best way I can explain it is "All That Is," this Center Point or Formless Intelligence behind life, creates everything out of Itself. Nothing can be separate from it. What this means is All That Is is having an experience of *itself* through us—*through our human nature.* In other words, one side isn't "better" than the other. When I finally came to this understanding, I started to respect and accept my human nature more with all of its faults, imperfections, and sometimes stupid things that I've done as a learning experience about the other side of the coin—my Spiritual Nature or my True Nature.

This "continuing education" of both sides of the coin is an ongoing process for each and every one of us. In the meantime, it's foolish to pass judgment on ourselves. We need to allow ourselves the freedom to make mistakes until we have a better understanding.

The way it works is that through our humanness or our human nature, our True Nature or our spiritual nature informs us though **wisdom** so that we can grow and evolve. They are always working together perfectly. It's a beautiful, built-in system.

Unlike what we've been led to believe, this Center Point or Formless Intelligence behind life does not have any inherent morality or apparent point of view. Any morality or point of view we have attached to it comes from our personal beliefs, our religion, and our culture. In other words, they are all made up.

This perfect Formless Intelligence behind life is also impersonal. By that I mean it does not have a preference on how we should live our lives. It allows us to decide our preference through the gift of free will.

You cannot decide how someone should live their life and give them free will at the same time. That is illogical. By giving us the gift of free will it allows us to choose our preferences. And in choosing our preferences we will always know whether we are moving *toward* or *away* from that Center Point through our life experiences. Negative experiences show us we are moving *away* from it. Positive experiences show us we are moving *toward* it.

Through the gift of free will we are allowed to have a human experience so that we can learn more about ourselves spiritually. This means making mistakes. Some of them will be small, some of them will be big, and occasionally some may even be horrible, but they are perfect mistakes because they are teaching you something that you can use to build a better life for yourself and others.

And, in the process, there's no judgment or punishment for our mistakes (other than cause and effect) because this impersonal Formless Intelligence or Center Point is an energy of unconditional love.

Unconditional love is a very difficult concept for human beings to accept because most of our love is conditional. Conditional love is based on the concept that I will love you if, when, until, and as long as you do this or that. But as you get into alignment with your Authentic Self and your True Nature you will come to realize that we are created out of a perfect Formless Intelligence of unconditional love that is beyond all these concepts.

Now how do we know that? From my perspective, it seems self-evident. When a child is born, we can clearly see it is a manifestation of pure, unconditional love. That's because unconditional love is our default setting. So, if we arrive here in the vibration of unconditional love, then we must come from the vibration of unconditional love. Thus, this perfect Formless Intelligence must be pure, unconditional love. And because it doesn't have an ego (the ego is part of our human nature), it loves you unconditionally.

Let's go back to the principle of gravity. Gravity doesn't care whether you believe in it or not. You don't get rewarded if you are a believer and you don't get punished if you're a non-believer. Gravity is just being gravity. It couldn't care less about what you believe.

This impersonal Formless Intelligence behind life operates in the same way. It doesn't care if you pay attention to it or not, or if you believe in it or not. It will always love you because its True Nature is unconditional love—and like gravity, it's always going to hold you up.

In fact, because it loves you so unconditionally, it will even allow you to believe you are not unconditionally loved! That's how unconditionally loved you are! It will even allow you to believe it doesn't exist. It gives you the freedom to decide what's true for you because it is experiencing *itself* through your unique perspective.

That's the whole idea behind Creation. "All That Is," this perfect Formless Creative Intelligence behind life, is experiencing itself through our unique perspectives. Otherwise, why bother to create you and me and everything else in the universe? Essentially, it's saying, "I am creating you out of myself so that you can have your own experience. And through your experience I will experience another aspect of myself and all creation."

So, in essence, each and every one of us are co-creators with this perfect Formless Creative Intelligence.

When you are in alignment with your Authentic Self, who you are beyond the physical aspect of you, you are automatically in alignment with "All That Is." That's when the magic begins to happen because you're also in alignment with reality.

Living in Alignment with Your Authentic Self

So how do we live in alignment with our Authentic Self? It's actually quite simple and natural. We're in alignment with our Authentic Self when we're living our highest **joy**, our **passion**, our **love,** and our **creativity**.

Those four things will allow you to live your magic and stay in alignment with your Authentic Self. Your highest *joy,* your *passion,* your *love,* and your *creativity* are about pursuing what makes you feel good and what comes naturally to you—and letting those things attract the things you desire in life.

Everything I do in my life is because it is part of my highest joy, my passion, my love, and my creativity. I don't teach, write, motivate, or entertain because I want to impress people. I do it because I am passionate about connecting with people. I love connecting with people in different ways and learning about their lives and seeing how I can help, or maybe just inspiring them a little—but ultimately, I'm doing it for myself.

And that's key number one. Whatever you do, don't do it for anyone else, or do it because you feel like that's what you're supposed to do, or it will make you a lot of money. Do it for yourself and others will benefit from it.

For example, there are a number of things I can do that will make money, which is often the underlying motivation for a lot of people. But the problem with doing anything just for the money is that you are always going to struggle with obtaining it, managing it, or living in fear of losing it.

When you pursue your highest *joy,* your *passion,* your *love,* and your *creativity* not just for the money but because you love to do something, the money will come automatically because people will see that you love what you do. They will also see that you're very good at it so they will gladly pay you whatever you ask which will allow you to live an abundant life.

What Does "Abundance" Really Mean?

Before we continue, let's stop for a moment and take a look at the word "Abundance." Most people when they think of abundance think of money, but abundance is more than money. Here's a definition of abundance that I'd like you to consider:

Abundance is the ability to attract *what* you need *when* you need it.

Notice there was no mention of money in that definition because there are so many ways in which abundance can show up. If you focus just on money, you will continue to struggle because you will shut down all of your other resources.

Now, abundance can come in the form of money, but if you believe that it must come in the form of money, you have a definition that focuses on money as the only doorway in which abundance can show up. By doing this, you're actually closing and locking all the other doors which will allow you to attract what you need when you need it. It shuts off or closes off all your other options because you refuse to identify or label those things equally as abundant as money.

Now when you allow *all* forms of abundance to be equal and equally valid, then whatever is the way or the path of least resistance for abundance to come to you will open up. It may be money, it may be a gift, or it may be something that synchronically happens from a person, event, or circumstance that allows you attract whatever you need when you need it.

Then moving forward and following your highest *joy*, your *passion*, your *love*, and your *creativity*, you can apply this idea or definition and trust that whatever form of abundance that needs to be there to allow you to attract whatever you need whenever you need it will be perfect—even if it doesn't show up in the way you expect or think it should. So, by expanding your definition of abundance, you also expand the ways that abundance can show up in your life.

Following the Path to Living Your Magic

There are many paths we can take to living our magic. However, before we embark on any path, we have to be careful about our intention. In other words, why are we choosing this particular path? This is a life lesson that I had to learn.

I started my career as a mental health professional or a therapist with a PhD. Along the way, I acquired a ton of training and certifications in almost every type of psychological and self-development training, including NLP, EFT, Hypnosis—you name it. I could paper an entire wall with all my degrees and certificates!

In the beginning, I used to do psychotherapy to help people to overcome their addictions and resolve their emotional issues. Looking back, I realize I got on this path for the wrong reason. I was trying to "save" people—to solve their problems and "fix" them.

Yet while all this was going on, my Inner Being or my Authentic Self was leading me to a new understanding. What I finally came to realize was that my role in life, in my work and in my relationships, is to **empower** and **inspire** people rather than trying to save or fix them. When I started focusing on empowering and inspiring people instead of trying to save them or fix them, everything changed.

Sharing Insight vs. Sharing a Map

In the process of doing this I got caught up in several psychological and spiritual teachings and methodologies. Most of them were before I had this understanding that I am sharing with you.

Over the years, I taught and shared these teaching and methodologies with other people. It is quite obvious to me now that some of the things I taught and shared in the past are different than what I believe today. The reason for this is that everything I said and taught in the past was based on a "map" I was living by at that time, but like any map, over time, it becomes out of date.

When I think about what I taught at that stage of my personal evolution, I realize I was unintentionally misleading some people because of my misunderstanding of how life actually works. That's the problem with any teaching. As a teacher, you put out a map of what the world looks like to you at that time, but the map is often out of date by the time people read it or experience it.

And I have to be honest with you: there are times when wish I could take back some of the things I used to teach. But I also realize that's part of my evolution. Because all you've got is what you see until you see something different. That doesn't mean there isn't value in my other work. Underneath the maps I've shared, there are principles. Principles are not belief systems. They're like gravity. Whether we agree with them or not, they are constant and unchangeable and always play a part in shaping our reality.

If there were not unchanging universal constants or principles, there would be relatively little value in writing or teaching. So, there's tremendous value in my other work. And if this book never came into existence, people could still benefit from my previous work for years to come.

So, the question you may be asking is, "How is what I teach now different than what I taught in the past?"

In other words, does this *replace* the teachings in my early work?

If I look at my past work, the underpinning philosophy of everything I taught was about changing our thinking, beliefs, and behaviors and what strategies, steps, and techniques we need to do or practice to achieve our desired outcome.

I used to think—not illogically—that since our experience of life is really an experience of our own thoughts that learning to control or manage our thinking is the most important thing we could learn to do.

The first part of my life was spent doing just that. I learned how to change the *content* of my thinking by using mind control techniques, affirmations, etc. I learned how to change the *structure* of my thinking by using techniques such as NLP, Clean Language, etc. And I learned how to change the *volume* of my thinking by using techniques such as mindfulness and meditation.

Every one of them was something I had studied and had put to use in my life. And they all worked and will still work! However, I found there's a much *easier* way.

Everything I learned and taught in the past was based on the idea that if it was going to be, it was up to me. For years, I found this a comforting idea because it seemed to give me more control over my life—or so I thought. But each time the universe kicked me to the curb and life didn't deliver what I demanded using these techniques and strategies, it also led to an incredible amount of pressure, stress, and self-doubt.

Trying to control my life by continually applying these techniques and strategies just led to more pressure, more stress, and more self-doubt. When I'm in this mindset, essentially, I am trying to borrow confidence from my past successes or use my intellect to convince myself I am in control when, in truth, there are too many variables I have no control over.

Then something interesting happened. I began to have a deeper understanding of how life actually works and how we often get in our own way. This allowed me to step back more and more and stop resisting "what is." In doing so, I began to have an understanding that while the results I want may or may not be in the cards, all I needed to do was focus on my desire and let things unfold naturally without trying to force the outcome. And what I discovered is that this is not only the best, but the most enjoyable way to live.

This approach, meaning I have really no control over the outcome of *anything* in my life, has left me free to accept "what is" and know I am going to be okay. How do I know that? Because I am still here! And so are you! No matter what has happened in your life, you're *still here*. You're okay.

But for some reason we have this idea that we need to struggle or try force the outcome of almost every situation in our life. However, knowing that I cannot control the outcome of anything has allowed me to let go of all that thinking about how things are supposed to turn out and simply stop trying to force the universe to live up to my expectations. And when I do this—when get out of my own way—I always end up with an outcome that is right for me. It's always at *right place*, at the *right time,* and with the *right people*. And, it's so much easier!

Another major difference between what I share now and what I taught in the past is how much work transforming my life used to look like to me compared to how simple it is now. I began to have an insightful understanding that there's a simple, natural way to live our lives without most of these personal development strategies, therapies, steps, methodologies, or techniques, or anything we need to do or practice to make the changes we desire in our life.

Now, I realize this is counterintuitive to most people because we're taught that when our lives are not working, there must be something "wrong" with us and we need to "fix" ourselves; thus, the need for self-improvement, self-development, and therapy. However, there's a much more natural way to change our lives if we understand our True Nature and how we create and shape our reality moment-to-moment.

A Major Reality Check—The Way It Works
One of the biggest challenges for people is to be introduced to new ideas that conflict with something they already believe is true. That's because we're all experts on how we see the world. We each have a model of how we think the world works, but often that model is out of alignment with reality.

Here's what you need to know: the extent to which we're not living a magical life and experiencing happiness, success, abundance, peace of mind, love, and connection is directly proportional to the degree with which we're not seeing how life actually works.

The Way Life Doesn't Work
Let's look at the way life doesn't work. When I first began to understand the true nature of reality and how it's actually created, it changed the way I constructed my life.

Here's the way I saw it before. Take a look at Diagram 1.

On the right side of the diagram is "life" or the "world"—the stuff "out there," that thing we're all living in.

I am on the left side of the diagram. (I went on a diet, so I was very thin!)

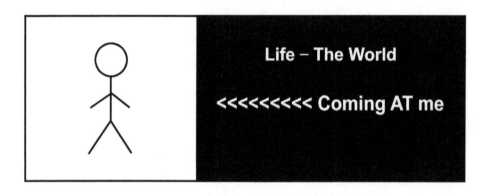

I believed that things that were happening in my life or in the world "out there" caused me to feel a certain way. If someone was mean to me, they caused me to feel upset. If I enjoyed a movie or a meal, it was a good movie or a good meal. If I didn't enjoy it, it was a bad movie or a bad meal.

If someone agreed with me, we could be friends. If not, I got upset. If someone rejected or insulted me, I felt hurt. If there were economic or political disasters, they affected the way I felt. If my bank balance or my business was up or down, it caused me to feel secure or insecure.

The list is endless.

In short, I was *externally driven* and reacted totally to the world "out there" because I believed that what was happening "out there" caused me to feel the way I do "in here," i.e. inside of me. This included not only the present, but my past as well. Essentially my understanding of how we create and shape our reality from the **outside-in** was a complete **misunderstanding**.

The Way Life Actually Works

Take a look at Diagram 2. What I've come to understand is that whatever I am feeling in any moment is not happening *to* me but coming *from* me. In other words, I am creating my reality from the **inside-out**, not the outside-in!

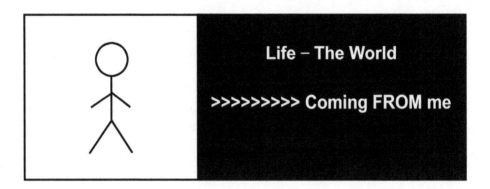

The way it actually works is that we have thinking going on in our head all day long automatically. That thinking is built into our psychological system. I am constantly thinking from the moment I am born until the moment I die. And my thinking constantly fluctuates. Sometimes it's positive, secure, optimistic, and happy and sometimes it's negative, pessimistic, insecure, or unhappy.

And the interesting thing is that because I feel the *effects* of my thinking in my body, I have a sensory perception that what's happening "out there" in the world is happening in me when, in truth, I see the world based on my thought-generated perception in the moment.

The happiness or unhappiness you experience in your life will always be in direct proportion to the insightful understanding you have concerning the true nature of reality: **100 percent of your felt experience of life is coming from your thought in the moment.** It is *never* coming from anything or anyone "out there" in the world. However, it doesn't always look that way so it's easy to get fooled.

Our experience of life moment-to-moment will almost always look like it's coming from "out there." For example, two people can be sitting side-by-side watching the same movie in a theater but they each have their own unique experience of the movie. What each one is feeling about the movie is coming from their thought-generated experience in the moment. So, when they come out of the movie and you ask each one how they enjoyed movie, one may say it was fantastic and the other may say they thought it was boring or it was too long or too short. It's like they were watching two different movies! But what's really happening is they each had their own unique experience of the movie. But neither experience is "real." Both are made-up.

In other words, the world "out there" doesn't actually exist for "me" until something happens *inside* of me, as I think about it and I give *meaning* to it. So, whatever I am feeling is coming *from* me, not *at* me.

This is true for all of us. It's not a belief, a theory, or anything we need to prove. It is self-proven. Our experience of life is always being generated from the inside-out—100 percent of the time—even when it doesn't look like it.

This **outside-in illusion** can be a frustrating way to live. Some people live there a lot of the time and others only occasionally, but we all fall into the trap of thinking we live in an outside-in world from time to time. When we think our feelings are coming from something other than our thinking in the moment, it massively complicates our lives. Let's look at a few common examples of how this outside-in illusion works.

The first example is when we have a belief that habits such as smoking, overeating, substance abuse, alcohol, etc. will change the way we feel.

Smoking, overeating, substance abuse, alcohol, and other habitual behaviors are common ways people try to deal with their feelings of anxiety and insecurity in the moment.

Let's look at smoking in particular. You hear people say, "I smoke because it de-stresses me." But their smoking habit is grounded in a couple of misunderstandings.

Misunderstanding #1: When people smoke to reduce stress, it looks as though their feelings of stress are coming from something other than their thinking in the moment. It's coming from their job, their partner, their finances, etc., but it doesn't work that way. In reality, 100 percent of their feelings of stress are coming from their thinking in the moment.

Misunderstanding #2: It looks as though their feelings of relief and relaxation are coming from the cigarette, but it doesn't work that way either. In reality, they think the cigarette is helping them to relax, but 100 percent of their feelings of relief and relaxation are coming from the thinking they attach to smoking. This works the same for overeating, substance abuse, alcohol, etc.

As a person increases their understanding of where their experience is actually coming from, they have a greater choice about what they do and don't do. Unhealthy habits often fall away because as your understanding increases, *your misunderstanding-based stress levels* decrease.

The second example of an outside-in illusion is the belief that we can enjoy our life more by changing our outside circumstances.

While we all have our ups and downs, life is inherently enjoyable. It's part of our default setting. But this isn't necessarily evident when we're confused about where our feelings of enjoyment come from. A quick scan of articles about "how to enjoy life more" reveals that even those who write articles are confused about the *source* of our feelings. Here are some of the most popular things they recommend: find a hobby you enjoy, read a book, do Yoga, meditate, listen to music, take a walk in nature, exercise more, get a pet, eat healthy, have more sex, get a good night's sleep, etc.

While all of those things may seem like good ideas, they have no causal connection to our enjoyment of life because 100 percent of our enjoyment of life comes from our thinking in the moment. In other words, none of them can make you *feel* anything that isn't *already* in your thinking.

The important point here is that we are never living in the feeling of our circumstances. We are always living in the feeling of our thinking in the moment.

- Feelings of **stress** come from our thinking in the moment
- Feelings of **dissatisfaction** come from our thinking in the moment
- Feelings of **enjoyment** come from our thinking in the moment
- Feelings of **love** come from our thinking in the moment

The enjoyment of life is our "default setting." It's what's there when there's nothing else in the way. And what gets in the way? The mistaken belief that we're feeling something other than our thinking in the moment.

The third example of an outside-in illusion is that finding the "right partner" will make us happy.

There is nothing wrong with wanting to find a partner to share your life with. Where people become stuck is when they mistakenly believe their feelings of happiness, joy, love, etc. can come from their partner. In fact, if you expect another person to make you feel *anything*, you're in for a huge disappointment.

Partner-seekers often run a pattern that goes like this: "I'll be happy when I find the right partner." And it's not just confined to partner-seekers; most people's goals have the same structure …

"I'll be (X) when I get (Y)." (X) is the feeling state and (Y) is the goal.

Here are a few more examples:

- I'll feel good about myself when I get fit.
- I'll feel secure once I have "X" number of dollars in the bank.
- I'll be happy when I get that new car.

- I'll be happy when I own my own home.
- I'll feel better once I find the right job, get that promotion, or start my own business.

Once again, it just doesn't work that way. We live in an inside-out world where 100 percent of our feelings come from our thinking in the moment and 0 percent of our feelings come from anywhere else.

Finding a compatible partner, having more money, getting fit, purchasing a new car or a home, getting a promotion, or starting your own business are all worthwhile goals but none of them make you feel anything that isn't already in your thinking.

The difference is this: when we feel insecure, we look outside of ourselves for something or someone to make us feel better or more secure. But when we know where our security comes from, we just want what we want knowing that it can enhance our life, but it can't make us *feel* anything.

The key understanding is that we are always living in the feeling of our thinking. We are never living in the feeling of our circumstances. Whether we are feeling excitement, love, happiness, frustration, longing, or disgust, they all seem to be directly connected to the outside world or our circumstances, but, in truth, they are simply reflections of whatever thoughts are passing through our mind in the moment.

The outside-in misunderstanding or illusion is one of the most important life lessons you will ever learn. If you understand the truth behind it, you will never be tricked again into believing that anything or anyone is the cause of how you feel or how you experience life.

Once you experience an increase in your level of understanding of the inside-out nature of life, you never lose it. You will still be tricked by it from time to time (I still am!), but it's only a matter of time, sometimes just minutes, before your innate intelligence kicks in and guides you back to sanity once again.

Chapter 3

THE ULTIMATE MAGIC TRICK

Since the title of this book is *Living Your Magic*, let's get into this a little deeper using magic as a metaphor.

The misunderstanding we have is when we think about things—our circumstances, our past, people, events, etc.—while we're doing it, it looks like those people, circumstances, or events, past or present, are causing us to feel the way we do, but as you have already learned, that's a profound reversal of the way it actually works.

It's similar to a magic trick. Magic is based on illusion. A magic trick works because of misdirection. The magician initiates a train of thought in the mind of the spectator based on a false assumption or perception. The sensation, surprise, and delight are created the moment the illusion or false train of thought is accepted by the spectator. Once the spectator has accepted the false assumption, they "buy into" the illusion as though it is real.

Due to a trick of the mind, our thinking and perception work just like a magic trick. And because it's like a magic trick, our perception always looks real to us—even if it's an illusion. The illusion is that what we're feeling is coming from the outside-in. But the secret behind this trick of the mind is that our feelings *always* come from the inside-out.

Our feelings are coming from our thought-generated perception in the moment, but like a good magic trick, the illusion can be very compelling. However, it's still a trick because it never works that way. How we feel inside is never generated from the outside by our past, our present, or our anticipated future.

When you don't understand how it works, it works like a magic trick. And then it's easy to get fooled. And thought is the ultimate magic trick. And because we're used to looking at the *effects* of our thoughts, we never see the trick. What we're learning here is to look at our life *before* the trick or the illusion happens. We're looking at where the trick comes from.

One of the insights I like to share with people is what I call the "First Transformative Truth." It's the idea that we don't live in the world as it is; we live in the world as it occurs to us. And how it occurs to us is *not* how it is. It's simply how we're making it up to be in that moment.

In any given moment, part of our mind is always in a hypnotic trance. What we experience as "reality" is filtered through our trances. And because of this, we never, ever get to experience reality as it is. Instead, we experience the world based on our thought-generated perception or the filter that we're looking through in the moment.

In that trance state, we are using our imagination to think and believe that what we see "out there" in the world is real. Yet, each one of us is making up our own version of reality or how we see the world.

What most people forget is that we don't see with our eyes. Our eyes are receivers. Our eyes receive light and it gets translated in our brain, but it's our mind that sees. It's our mind that's perceiving reality. Another way of way of saying this is that seeing through our mind is like wearing a pair of glasses. What we're really seeing is just a projection of our mind filtered through our glasses. The problem is that if we have the wrong prescription, our entire view of the world will be distorted or out of focus. What this means is that what we're seeing is not reality, but our thought-generated perception of reality. And this is why seeing is not believing, but, in fact, believing is seeing. Whatever we believe is what we will see.

It's Always the Same Problem and the Same Solution

If you understand you're creating everything in your world moment-by-moment through your thoughts, it also shifts an inherent misunderstanding that what you've created in the *past* is the cause of how you feel in the *present*. The problem lies in feelings you have *about the past in this moment*, not what happened in the past.

Most traditional psychology is based on the premise that when we're stuck, our problem or our situation is usually rooted in our past experiences. In order to find the solution, it focuses on our personality, our ego, and the experiences we've had in the past. It teaches that the way you "fix" people is to go into their past and try to help them resolve their past issues so they can move forward. In other words, the past happened to us and it affects our life now, so we need to address it.

The idea of delving into our past and understanding how our past affected us is left from the legacy of Freud, which dominated psychology for many years. It operates from a flawed premise. Essentially, it means looking *backwards* while trying to move *forwards*. But the real problem is that while we're doing that, our *new* reality is being created in this moment! This is where our focus needs to be, simply because we no longer have any control over what happened in the past. It's over. But we have *full control* of how we choose to feel in this moment.

I was unwittingly educated exactly the opposite by everyone who was making this same mistake. The understanding of how reality is actually created moment-to-moment changed my psychological understanding from a circumstance, situation, and past-based psychological approach to a psychology based on *how we are creating and shaping our reality moment-to-moment.*

This past-based psychology is so entrenched into our culture that often when I work with someone, that's what they expect. They are convinced that in order for me to understand them and help them, we must go into their past. And unless I tick off that box, it's often difficult for them to give themselves permission to change. In these situations, I take them into the past and address it quickly. And as long as I do that, even for a few minutes, they are satisfied. Then I get them back into the present moment as quickly as possible so we can do the real work.

Also, the other missing piece for me was understanding our True Nature or the Spiritual Mechanism behind life and behind our thinking. You cannot have one without the other. The attempt to choose psychology, which focuses on your thinking and ignores your spirituality which is your connection with the deeper Intelligence behind life, or visa-versa, is like trying to choose between two cars: one without an engine and one without a steering wheel. Trust me, you're not going anywhere while trying to use either one of them! You cannot have one without the other.

What I've come to understand is that every psychological and spiritual problem we face in life stems from the same two things:

1. A misunderstanding of how we individually and collectively are participating in creating our reality moment-to-moment.
2. How we are individually and collectively out of alignment with our Authentic Self and the deeper Intelligence behind life.

That's it! And if both of these things are healed, all the rest of our so-called problems, issues, and addictions go away by themselves! If our life is problematic and we're struggling, it's because we're caught up in a misunderstanding of one or both of these two universal principles.

A universal principle is something that's true for all people at all times, regardless of their psychological or religious beliefs. They are about who we are and how life works. This is important because as we understand more about who we are and how life works, it alters the way we experience ourselves and the world around us. The foundations on which we build our lives become more solid because they're rooted in reality before the formation of our own individual beliefs.

Before I insightfully understood those two principles, I was caught up in a misunderstanding of who I was and my True Nature. And as result, I thought I was broken. I was living from an Illusory made-up Self that was not "real." And that Illusory made-up Self was the Self I was trying to fix, change, and improve.

I had this full-time job of trying to "improve" myself, to be spiritual, to be worthy, to be accepted by others, to achieve success, etc. Then I finally realized that when I'm in touch and in alignment with my Authentic Self, there's nothing to worry about, nothing to fix, nothing to change, nothing to improve, and nothing to develop. What a relief!

That's when it occurred to me that we got it all wrong and the very idea of self-improvement and self-development makes no sense if there's no "Self" to improve or develop! Why improve who you are if who you are—your Authentic Self—is one and the same with this deeper Intelligence behind life? An Intelligence which is pure creative potential. What's there to improve? If that's the *starting point*, how are you going to improve on that? So, the solution is simple. All you have to do is start living from your Authentic Self instead of your Illusory made-up Self or your ego.

So instead of trying to fix people, I realized I could empower them by helping them to see they are not psychologically damaged or broken and they don't need to be fixed. In the past, when people would come to me, I would try to solve their problem or their issue and base my "treatment" or "therapy" on their symptoms. I used to think about what technique, strategy, or methodology I would use to help them.

Once I had this new understanding, I knew that when someone came to me, whatever problem or issue they came with was just a misunderstanding of one or both of those two principles. This is what we need to focus on first. But until we understand our True Nature, how our reality is actually created moment-to-moment and how to access the deeper wisdom of our Authentic Self, it will make sense to you, like it did to me, to use these prescriptive therapies, techniques, and strategies.

So, I changed my approach. Instead of sharing my best map, I prefer to point people to their own deeper wisdom and their own insights so that they don't need my map. And what I like best about this approach is how much more enjoyable it is to point people towards those things so that they can learn to trust the deeper wisdom that's already built within them.

In other words, rather than looking to others for advice or following contradictory psychological, spiritual, or religious teachings from thousands of years ago, or even last year, or last week, or follow somebody else's teaching that's going to be out of date as well, we need to learn to trust the deeper wisdom and Intelligence flowing through us.

We are not designed to need any spiritual, religious, or psychological teaching outside of ourselves to create true happiness, connection, and well-being because everything we need to know is part of our default setting! We came here with this knowledge already built within us.

So now I help people to understand that they know more than they think they know and that they are not psychologically damaged or broken. All the work I do now, which includes this book, is about deconstructing people's "realities" and helping them to see that **all that's really going on is they are making up the world they live in and then either enjoying or suffering from what they made up.**

Of equal value is when people come to see that they are making up the world they live in, they have the opportunity to make it up in ways that work *for* them instead of *against* them. Once we see that the world we live in is made up from *our memory and our imagination*, we realize that we don't have to settle for what we think we can have. We can play at creating anything we desire, even if it seems impossible.

My job is to help people see the unconscious limitations they are not aware of or are invisible to them so they can go back to their default setting of innate wisdom and access the deeper Intelligence within them and do things differently. I help them to see they are just living with a misunderstanding of how they are creating their reality, who they truly are, and where their power is coming from. And once we understand that on a deeper level, it's remarkably easy to change anything about our life almost immediately and live the life we prefer.

It's freeing for me and the people I work with because it's always going to be the same thing. It's always going to be about the way we are thinking about something in the moment and the way we're creating a story and making that story "real."

The difference in what I do now and what I've done in the past is that now I look at the innate mental health in people and don't get caught up in their story. It's not that I don't feel empathy for what they are going through now or have gone through in the past, or I'm trying to dismiss it or say they can forget about it, but they don't need to keep thinking about it over and over again!

I tell them, "The more you keep thinking about it, the more it's going to continue to grow out of proportion, which is going to make it more difficult for you to let go. If you think of a snowflake, it lands, it melts, and it's gone. Another one lands, it melts, and it's gone. But if there's a *snow storm* and the snowflakes keep piling up, you've got a heavy pile of snow and it's going to be much harder to move."

The snow storm is a metaphor for the **thought storm** they have about their situation. Then I say, "Can you see that's what you're doing? You're not allowing those thoughts about your past or your situation to melt away. You're just packing one thought on top of another."

When they want to talk about the negative, undesirable, or even traumatic situations in their past or what has happened to them, I often say, "If you watched a movie that was really disturbing and it made you feel bad, would you watch it again?"

And they say, "No."

"Then why do you keep going over and over that past event again and again? What are you getting out of it?"

They usually respond by saying, "I never thought about it that way."

I can clearly see that's what they're caught up in, but I refuse to "buy into" it and I'm not believing that's all they are, that's all they have, or that they're stuck where they are. Why? Because I understand their True Nature and I'm focusing on their **innate mental health**, rather than focusing on their problem or their issue.

Our True Nature is Innate Mental Health

Traditional psychology and mental health professionals assume when a client or patient comes to them, they are experiencing some form of mild to severe mental illness. However, I prefer to take a different approach. Instead of using the "mental illness" model, what if we saw everyone as already having innate mental health?

I prefer to operate from the model that innate mental health is our default setting. It's not something we have to work towards. It's not a goal or a place to get to because you're *already there*! The problem is that you don't know it because you're caught up in a misunderstanding of how you're creating your reality moment-to-moment.

What I have found is that once people realize that they already have innate mental health, but they're not seeing it as a reality, it opens the door to a solution so simple that most people often miss it. They begin to understand that they're not seeing or experiencing it because they believe if they can *have a thought about something*, which in their case is their problem or issue, it must be real or true. This belief is the very thing that is creating the reality they are trying to get rid of and are being treated for. What they're missing is that *they are making up their thoughts,* which is at the root cause of their problem.

I'm not saying this approach is 100 percent foolproof, but I am saying that it works 100 percent better than anything I've ever used. However, most therapeutic approaches operate from the "mental illness" model which assumes the client or patient is psychologically damaged or broken. Their solution is designed to try to "fix" or "cure" their perceived mental illness through talk therapy, behavioral change, and pharmaceutical intervention.

In cases of Bipolar, Manic Depressive, Schizophrenia, or any other type of mental disorders where the client or patient is out of control or might hurt themselves, specific types of therapeutic approaches and medication can be quite effective.

However, the real problem is that the psychiatric profession, together with the pharmaceutical companies, have convinced us that the best temporary solution to our psychological problems, including mild depression, stress, and anxiety, is by altering our brain chemistry through the use of prescription drugs.

We often see medical doctors and psychiatrists prescribe antidepressants to patients when their anxiety levels get high or when they exhibit symptoms or behaviors that didn't work for them in the past. That's not a mental disorder! That's just getting caught up in our thinking in the moment! It happens to all of us—and it's "normal."

The wide distribution of antidepressants has now become the default approach to a large majority of mental health issues. This is evidenced by the fact that psycho-pharmaceutical medication of the general population has increased over 200 percent in the past ten years.

Another alarming statistic is the massive increase in children from ages ten to fourteen who are now being prescribed antidepressants. We even have toddlers on antidepressants. Recently I met a young woman in her late twenties who has been on antidepressants for almost a decade! Yet, when she was first prescribed them, she was suffering from anxiety in primary school!

So, your argument might be, "What about people who feel better after taking these medications?" Duh! That's like asking, "What about people who feel better after they take heroin or cocaine?" Of course they're going to feel better for a while, but the medication is only masking the problem.

Yet, there is not one tiny bit of evidence that suggests that antidepressants will change the *cause* of any mental disorder. This is why so many people relapse into their previous condition after taking these medications. In the end, they are destroying their brain and their body.

The pharmaceutical approach turns *normal people* into *patients* by making them dependent on an outside force: pills dispensed by a benevolent physician or psychiatrist. In most cases, emotional problems that could be solved by one's own skills, understanding, and actions are literally chemically turned off and turned over to an outside agent for the solution.

Most of these psychological symptoms, such as anxiety, stress, and mild depression, that are being treated with medication are not neurologically or biochemically related. They come from the mind. The mind is creating the symptom. How do I know this? I know this because I can replicate every single symptom experienced by a patient who is diagnosed with any "mental illness" just by using hypnosis. And, I can do this just using language and nothing else. Think about that!

Don't believe me? Go watch a hypnosis stage show where people will have positive or negative hallucinations such as seeing the audience naked when everyone in the audience has their clothes on. Or, getting them to forget their name, or even where they are. Even projecting them to another planet and have them speak an alien language that doesn't exist. My point is that the effect or symptom they're experiencing is *not biochemically induced.* There is no brain disorder. All the hypnotist is doing is using language to create their behavior.

What would happen if people really understood that the *root cause* behind almost every psychological problem we face is a thought we are making up and believing it is real. What if we really understood that most of our anxiety, stress, and depression would dissipate almost immediately if we stopped "buying into" our thinking in the moment?

If we really insightfully understood that, our entire collection of coping and avoidance strategies would come to an immediate end as well. It would no longer be necessary to medicate ourselves with alcohol to avoid the pain of our thoughts. We could turn off the loud music that drowns out our thinking. Overeating, compulsive dieting, and smoking would no longer be necessary to give ourselves temporary relief. Anorexia, bulimia, and a never-ending series of cosmetic surgeries and tattoos would no longer be necessary for us to feel better about our body.

We could toss the antidepressants and illegal substances into the rubbish because we no longer need the effect they artificially produce. We would no longer need any of them because the source behind all of them would become apparent.

What if we could see that whatever feelings we have about anything or anyone are based on our thought in the moment? And if we don't "buy into it," it will die its own death and leave us alone, free to enjoy our mind and enjoy our life!

How do we know this is true? We know this is true because there are other people who have the *same problems and same situations* in their lives as we do, but they don't have the *same feelings or reactions* that we have. They don't need any medication because they are not caught up in their thinking and believing that just because they can have a thought about something, whether it's their past, present, or future, it must be true!

This understanding can be highly beneficial to all of us, especially for people who are often misdiagnosed with mental health problems when all that's really happening is a misunderstanding of how they are creating their reality through their thought in the moment.

All the work I do today is based on waking people up to that fact that they're making up their own world through thought. Not so that they can stop thinking completely, or substitute one made-up reality for another, but so that they wake up to their True Nature: innate mental health.

The Subtractive Approach vs. the Additive Approach

Most therapeutic interventions and even self-development programs are based on the premise that there's something "wrong" with our thinking and to some degree we are psychologically broken. The role of the therapist, coach, or self-development guru is to help to put us back together again. Their solution usually involves using an "additive" approach.

We're all suckers for the additive approach. You see it everywhere from self-development books and courses to government interventions, crash diets, medications, get-rich-quick schemes, etc.

Take a look at any magazine and you will see headings like: "The 4 Keys To Building Muscle Fast" or "The 5 Sexual Moves That Will Make You Irresistible" and "6 Secrets of a Successful Relationship" or "10 Steps to Financial Freedom." It goes on and on.

The additive approach works on this formula: you + the additive approach = a better you.

When we're feeling insecure, additive approaches can be very compelling. That's why they're used as the primary driver behind almost every self-help, get-rich-quick, how-to-become-a-better-you, or how-to-become-a-more-beautiful-you course or book.

The additive approach is also used in most therapeutic interventions. In essence, you can become a "better you" by *adding* the information, strategy, methodology, or a technique you learned from the therapist that will help you to change your thinking and behaviour. And it works! But most of the time, it won't last.

To be perfectly honest, that's the way I looked at it for many years. However, I no longer see it this way. I prefer to use the subtractive approach.

This is the approach we will be using throughout this book. Instead of giving you more to process, what you're learning is designed to take things off your mind, giving you less to remember, less to think about, and less to do. It's about subtracting or taking away everything that's keeping you from understanding your True Nature and how your mind actually creates and shapes your reality moment-to-moment.

What you're left with is a clear mind in which there is little or no contaminated thinking to get in your way. When you have less on your mind and you subtract the misunderstandings you have about how life works and the true nature of reality, you can enjoy your mind and your life. And the best part is, it's self-proven. And because it's self-proven, there's nothing to believe. There are no techniques, strategies, NLP, psychological interventions, affirmations, or positive thinking. You just go out, live it, and prove it for yourself!

I have found over and over again when people use a subtractive approach rather than an additive approach they fall back into their default state of innate mental health. And when they do, it gives them permission to be themselves and frees them to choose a life path that's most in alignment with who they are.

So, I no longer take on the role of a therapist. Instead, I prefer to act as a friend who is not trying to "fix" them, because I know they are not broken. And once they "get" that, they have access to all the inner resources they need to change anything in their life. This frees them up to live their magic and have the life they want and deserve.

If I work with someone and they want to tell me what has happened to them in the past, that's fine, but I really don't need to know the details for one simple reason: it's not happening now! That's what I work with—how people are now—because the power to create the life we desire is not in the past. It's in the now.

My intention is to set a new baseline for their experience of life. I see it as a way of restoring their default settings. This allows them to experience less stress and less worry and have a more organic experience of life that enables them to truly create the life they're inspired to create. This is also my intention for you!

Self-Mentoring Through Deeper Intelligence

With this in mind, I switched from "therapy" to what I call "Self-Mentoring." The Self I am referring to is our Authentic Self.

You're probably familiar with a TV program called the "The Voice." Contestants compete for the best Voice of the season and win a large cash prize as well as a recording contract. If they're selected as one of the final contestants, they're paired up with a mentor who is one of the Voice judges.

They pair them up with mentors who have a lot of experience in the entertainment field. And guess what? They massively improve over the season because they're working with the mentor. Well, it's the same thing with us. We do better inside of ourselves no matter how well-developed our intellect and life experience is when we allow ourselves to be mentored by the deeper wisdom and Intelligence that comes from our Authentic Self.

If I don't know that I am connected to that deeper wisdom and Intelligence—if I don't know how it works through me—I am going to struggle. Not because I have to struggle, or because life is a struggle, but because I am operating with only a fraction of the inner knowledge and resources that are available to me.

If I *don't* understand this, I am going to feel I need all these psychological and spiritual teachings, techniques, therapies, and disciplines to make the changes in my life.

If I believe I'm disconnected from the flow, or there's no flow to disconnect from or connect to, it makes sense to rely on something or someone outside of me that can help improve my situation. Thus, the additive approach makes sense. But if I understand that everything I need comes from the deeper wisdom and Intelligence within me, I can just get out of the way and allow it to guide me, mentor me, and coach me moment-to-moment.

So, there's nothing I need to add. Rather, the innate wisdom and deeper Intelligence flowing from my Authentic Higher Self informs me moment-to-moment about what I need to subtract. This is why the subtractive approach is so powerful. There is nothing to fix, change, or improve. It's about subtracting and *letting go* of what's getting in our way. It's not about analyzing why it's there, but just letting it go. And in that space comes the wisdom from our Inner Mentor or our Authentic Self that allows us to resolve any issue or reach any goal. It also allows us to follow the natural path of least resistance that is most in alignment with who we are.

Chapter 4

DISCOVERING YOUR NATURAL PATH

There are a lot of people who feel like they don't know what to do with their lives. They don't know what path to follow. Chances are you have lots of ideas or things you may want to do, but you're not fully feeling it. It's like you're missing the inspiration that pulls you towards what you want to do.

In my case, I had a lot of options, but for a long time there wasn't a really strong pull toward any of them. This is because I wasn't following my natural talents and abilities.

We're all good at something that comes naturally to us. For some people it's working with their hands, for some people working with their mind, and for some it is expressing themselves through art or performance.

I'm hopeless working with my hands. Yet, I can watch a tradesperson build something and be completely fascinated by how he or she can cut that piece of wood or metal and have it fit perfectly.

I also love art, but I struggle to draw a stick figure! I can't even draw a straight line with a ruler!

I love music and tried to learn to play an instrument, but I'm hopeless at playing any musical instrument. Yet, when I watch someone play a musical instrument, I am fascinated.

I'm fascinated by how people can come up with scientific formulas or study the universe, nature, animals, etc. When I see them passionate about what they do, I am truly inspired.

When I watch people play sports who are extremely good at what they do, I am also inspired, even thought I was never good at playing any sports.

Like most people, at a deeper level, I knew I had natural talents and abilities that I wasn't tuning into. However, I was beginning to have a sense of what they were and what I wanted to do, but I have learned not to take any action unless I feel *inspired*, because if I'm inspired, I know I am going in the right direction.

So, I asked the inner wisdom of my Authentic Self, my Inner Mentor, "How can I bring forth my natural abilities, my highest joy, my passion, and my creativity?"

Intuitively, the answer was that I should inspire and entertain. And to be honest, I had no clue how I was going to do that.

I felt this was the direction I needed to take. However, I wasn't sure that this was the right path. The way I went about it was I asked myself this question—and this is an interesting question you can ask yourself—"If I just won the Lotto for 50 million dollars, if I had 50 million dollars right now and had everything I could possibly dream that money can buy and I travelled everywhere in the world I wanted to travel and got that out of my system, what would I do with the *rest of my life* in order to continue to feel like life mattered?"

Even if your life is perfect and you have everything money could possibly buy, you would have to keep doing something to continue to give *meaning* to your life, to feel your highest joy, your passion, and your creativity. I realized that if I had everything money could possibly provide, I love to inspire and entertain.

The Magician Shows Up!

As soon as I became clear on my intention, which was to inspire and entertain, something magical happened. I mean that literally! It began with a phone call from a guy who got in touch with me and he said, "I want to learn hypnosis. Can you teach me?" I had never taught hypnosis to anyone before, but my "Inner Mentor" or my Authentic Self was telling me to pursue it, so I said yes. He asked me how much, and I came up with a figure which was quite high considering he could have taken any number of hypnosis courses for a lot less.

He said, "Okay, that's fine."

Then I said, "You will need eight weeks of training and practice so I can evaluate you and fine-tune your skills." And he was okay with that too.

Then I asked, "What do you do for a living?"

He said he was a magician. I actually had never met a magician before, so I was intrigued.

He came to my office which was in my home and we sat down. I said to him, "So you're really a magician. Can you show me a magic trick?"

He takes a deck of cards out of his pocket and sets deck on the table and says, "Before I came here, I turned one card over in the deck. I want you to just think of any card out of fifty-two cards in the deck. Any card." So, I said the ten of hearts off the top of my head. He takes the deck out of the box and spreads the cards out and *only one card* in the deck is turned over. And—you guessed it—it was the ten of hearts!

I said, "That's insane, how did you do that?"

And he told me, "There is a magician's code where we promise not to reveal how a trick is done.

So, I asked him to do another trick.

He asked if I had a $5 note. I took it out of my wallet and handed it to him. He told me to check the serial number, so I did. He asked me, "If I was a real magician what would be the most impressive thing I could do with this $5 note?"

I told him he could turn it into a $100 note. He showed me his hands were completely empty and then right in front of me he folded up my $5 note and when he unfolded it, the $5 note was completely gone and in its place was a real $100 note.

He gave it to me for examination. I checked his hands and there was nothing there. He had short sleeves on, so it wasn't hidden up his sleeves either. Then he took back the $100 note. Now this time I was really watching him because I knew what to expect. He folded it again right in front of my face and turned it back into a $5 note. I checked the serial number and it was my $5 note! I was completely amazed—and I was hooked!

And then it hit me. This is something I want in my life. At that point, I had no idea how I was going to use it, but I knew it was a stepping stone and I was inspired to take action. Then I asked him if he wanted to swap skills: I would teach him hypnosis if he would teach me magic. We had a deal!

We worked together for eight weeks and I began to use what he taught me in my consulting practice to build rapport with my clients and it worked beautifully. I used magic to demonstrate how our mind can be influenced to create an *illusion* that looks real to us.

And it also added another dimension. My clients were having fun with me. Initially, before I learned magic, my approach was very serious. That's the way I was trained. When working with my clients I would often use academic, psychological terminology. Looking back retrospectively, I could see that my approach was too dense, so I became a recovering academic. I reminded myself that's not the way I choose to work with people. Regardless of how "serious" their problems are, if during my time with them they are not enjoying themselves and feeling better, then they are not transforming and I'm not being myself.

Let me give you an example. A client came to me because he was experiencing depression. So, I ask him, "How can I help you?"

He says, "I am totally depressed."

I said, "Really? What does totally depressed mean to you?"

He says, "Nothing but depression."

"Okay, you get up in the morning and your eyes open. How do you feel?"

He says, "I'm depressed."

"You go the bathroom and take a shower. How do you feel?"

"I'm depressed."

"Eating breakfast?"

"I'm depressed."

"Diving your car, going to the store?"

"I'm depressed."

He was totally invested in being depressed.

Then I asked, "Does this go on every day?"

And he says "Yes."

So, I do what is known in NLP as a "pattern-interrupt." I said, "You lucky bastard."

He goes "What?"

I said, "Do you know how difficult it is to maintain one state of mind that is powerful and true *all day every day*? I'm going to study you because people all over the world would do anything to have that skill."

He says, "But I'm depressed."

Then I told him, "That's because you're highly skilled at being depressed. You're really good at what you do. This shows me you can accomplish anything you want to if you put your mind to it. To maintain *one state of mind* all day every day for your entire life is not easy. You're a Jedi master!"

Then he starts to laugh. And as soon as he starts to laugh, I said, "Now quit lying to me."

He said, "What do you mean?"

"You're laughing right now and told me you're always depressed."

He starts laughing even more.

Now in the old days, after he told me he was depressed I would start in with all this academic, psychological terminology, but what I've learned is that having fun is the most powerful bridge to personal change. For me, it is the *starting point* of all personal change.

I don't care how serious a person's problem is, my job is to get them to shift their state. I often start with a magic trick. I also use humour and absurdity to shift people's state like I did with this guy who had depression.

And once I can see their state has shifted and they are enjoying themselves, the rest is easy because their subconscious gives up resistance to change when they're having fun so I can just drop whatever I want into their subconscious and the change becomes so much easier.

After I started doing this, my referral rate went through the roof because clients were telling their friends how much fun they were having with me and that they were feeling so much better.

I would also do this when I put them in hypnosis. I would have their arm and hand rise automatically to their head. As that was happening, I would say, "As that hand moves towards your head, you're going to experience an amazing sense of well-being." And as their arm continues to rise, I would say, "And that good feeling is turning into a smile. That's right. And as that hand gets closer to your head, that smile is turning into laughter. And when that hand touches your head, you will start laughing uncontrollably. There's nothing you can do about it."

And I just keep increasing it until they're laughing uncontrollably. Then I stick their hand to their head, and they laugh even more.

That's the last thing I want them to remember before they leave. I have had so many people say this experience alone was worth the cost of the entire session. They love it. So essentially everything I did from that point on was rooted in the idea of **conditioning with pleasure**. In fact, everything I do is centered on conditioning with pleasure rather than trying to change people's thinking or behavior.

As I began to do this, I had another realization. Although I enjoyed doing one-on-one change work and it was rewarding, I discovered my true *aliveness*, my highest *joy*, my *passion*, and my *creativity* comes from entertaining, inspiring, and teaching, so I decided that I would no longer do any type of therapy. There are plenty of people out there who love to do it, so I will leave it to them.

However, I still entertain, inspire, and teach but what I do now is pure performance art. I call it the "Pursuit of Astonishment." Astonishment is a feeling of joy and wonder that often comes from the unexpected. It is a powerful force that can create a great impact.

I loved the idea of being a magician, but to be honest, I didn't have the dexterity to do the moves, slights, and manipulation necessary to perform the tricks professionally. Instead, I decided to use my natural talents to become a "Mind Magician." As a Mind Magician, I use my training and experience in hypnosis, body language, suggestion, psychological persuasion, and the mystic arts to read people's thoughts, implant suggestions, predict their behavior, and literally tap into their mind! In fact, the name of my performance is "Mind Tapped."

What I do in private functions, theatre, and fundraisers is a mixture of illusion and my actual ability. So, in my performances, what I do is intentionally blur the lines between illusion and reality so that the audience or participants have no idea whether what they're seeing and experiencing is an illusion or my actual ability.

The purpose of that is to make people question. It makes them wonder what is possible. And that's my intention because I want people to discover what's possible for them. I want them to hold the questions: "Is it possible to use energy?" or "Is it possible to read peoples thoughts?" or "Is it possible to influence people?" and "Is it possible to connect with other people on a higher level than just verbally?" or "Is it possible to trust your intuition and innate wisdom to make the right decisions every single time?" and "Is it possible to attract synchronicity?"

And even when I use magic, it doesn't mean there aren't real ways to do those things.

My primary intention in all of this is to skillfully entertain my audience by bringing them into a world where they can temporarily forget their day-to-day reality and enjoy their mind. For me, there's a certain quality of healing that comes from making people feel good and have fun that no amount of self-help, coaching, therapy, or teaching can provide. And that's what the "Pursuit of Astonishment" is all about.

I now see myself as an "edu-tainer." I educate and entertain at the same time. The emphasis is on entertaining, but when people are having fun, their subconscious is open to receiving new ideas and inspiration. This allows me to drop some really cool stuff in there that will inspire them to look at the possibilities in their life instead of their imitations.

But here's the important point. Even though the one-on-one change work I was doing was rewarding, being an edu-tainer brings out my *aliveness*. Perhaps there is a message in here for you as well. Just because you are good at something doesn't mean you have to do it for the rest of your life. Perhaps it's time to follow your aliveness.

And there is something else to consider. If you do what you love and you do what comes natural to you, you will never work another day in your life. Period! Nothing I do now is work. Everything I do is effortless. Effortless means it comes naturally through synchronicity. And when it does, I just flow with it.

Giving Up a Lifetime of Struggle

According to Albert Einstein, one of the most important questions that that each person must answer for themselves is: "Is the Universe friendly?"

It seems a little unusual that a scientist like Einstein would imply that the Universe, the Formless Intelligence behind life, might have a bias. However, I think what he was asking is: "Are we designed to live a life of struggle, or to live a life without struggle?"

How we answer this question does make a big difference! After all, if we are designed to struggle, then life is going to be difficult. And, many people believe this. So, what's the actual truth about struggle? Before I give it to you, I need you to read the following statement:

Anytime I am struggling or feel resistance, it means I am going in the _wrong direction._

Please read it again.

One of the things I have fully come to understand about life is that if you're struggling or resisting anything, you're going in the _wrong direction._ So, if there's anything in your life that causes you some form of resistance, that frustrates you or that drains you, it simply means the deeper wisdom of your Authentic Self, your Inner Being, is trying to tell you that you're going in the wrong direction. On the other hand, if it's telling you the opposite, if something is easy and effortless, it's guiding you and telling you that you're going the right direction.

I know they teach you in the "School of Life" that without pain, there is no gain and you have to struggle to get what you want, but that's simply not true. The truth is that you _can_ gain without pain.

To live fully is to take the path of least resistance. Least resistance is living in the flow of life. And it's interesting to me that in all the work I have done with people over the years, that's what everyone really wants! They would come with all these problems, but if you dig deep enough, every single one of them just wants to have peace and live in the flow of life.

Whenever you're struggling or feeling resistance, it is time to stop doing what you're doing—immediately. Put simply, you should take no action on anything until you feel no resistance and it feels like your next step, whatever that is, is the most logical step.

How can you know if the next step is the most logical step? The way to know is when it feels like there is no effort, no strain, and no pain. This is using the leverage of energy, the same leverage of energy that creates everything in the Universe.

Have you ever seen people who seem to have all the wonderful things in their life without much effort? It almost seems like they have an advantage over everyone else. Then you see that people who work the hardest usually have the least. That doesn't seem fair, does it? But here's why. They are working hard and going about creating their lives the hard way because they don't understand the concept of leverage.

The simple definition of "leverage" is: to do more with less. The people who are working hard are trying to use their *actions* to create the outcomes in their lives. They haven't learned how to use the power of their mind to leverage or reduce their actions. When you understand how to leverage the power of your mind with your actions, you'll be able to accomplish more with less work, less effort, less energy, and without struggle.

Giving up the struggle also means giving up resistance because whatever you resist will continue to persist. Remember the war against poverty? How about the war against drugs? Now we have the war against terrorism. How's that working out? They're all doomed to failure because when we fight against or resist anything, it may go away for a while, but eventually it will attract more of what we're fighting against. This is called "push against" energy.

You can't get what you want by pushing against what you don't want. The way it works is that whatever we put our attention and emotional energy on—whether it is positive or negative—will eventually show up in our lives. The Universe or the Formless Intelligence behind life doesn't have a preference between positive or negative, good or bad, fear or courage, pessimism or optimism. It treats them exactly the same. If we're putting energy on it, or we're pushing against it, we're placing an order for it to show up in our lives.

Non-resistance is one of the most misunderstood principles of success. Non-resistance is simply taking the mental attitude that whatever *is*, just *is*, and we don't need to fight it or resist it.

Most of us go through life focusing on how things "are" and then compare them with how we think they "should be." This causes us to set up resistance to the behavior of people or circumstances that we can't do anything about. We say to ourselves (and others), "He shouldn't have done that!" or "That shouldn't have happened!" or "She shouldn't have treated me like that!" or "We should have won that contract!"

Sound familiar?

It probably does, because we've all done it! There are a couple of things to notice about this though. First, notice that we're pushing against and arguing with reality being the way it is! How successful do you think you're going to be when you push against or argue with reality?

Second, notice the thought pattern that goes with this. In our mind, someone or something has taken our "stuff"—our money, our success, our love, or our respect—or has hurt us in some way and now we are the victim. And as soon as we declare ourselves a victim of anything or anyone, we're stuck, because the simple truth is: *you cannot be a victim and be happy at the same time.* There's no such thing as a happy victim. You can choose one or the other, but you can't be both at the same time.

Perhaps you believe that you are a victim. And you may be "right," but you won't be happy as long you hold on to your victimization. Sometimes you have to make a choice. You can either be "right" about your victimization, or you can choose to be happy and let it go. In every single moment of your life, you are choosing one or the other.

A simple definition of insanity is to keep doing the same thing and expect a different result. So, in order to change, if any feeling or emotion is not getting you what you want, you need to let it go *right now*. Tell yourself, "I may be 'right,' and I may be 'justified' about the way I feel, but it's not getting me what I want. So, from now on, I choose to just let it go."

Non-resistance doesn't mean you have to be a doormat for anyone. It only means that you stop arguing with reality or "what is."

It is human nature to take a position on something and label it either good or bad, better or worse, fair or unfair as opposed to something else, but the moment you label a person, event, circumstance, or thing as being a certain way in your mind, you set up a reaction to it. For example, if you label an event as "disappointing," you instantly assume the position of resisting the disappointment because that's the way you labeled it. It's your thought-generated perception and the accompanying resistance that causes something to be experienced as disappointing.

The moment you surrender your position and let go of your resistance and consciously connect to the idea that everything is "just the way it is," then that person, event, circumstance, or thing ceases to be "disappointing." Your disappointment stems from your internal representation and the way you label it.

With conscious surrender to **what is**, virtually all the things that you regard as undesirable, including illness, financial setbacks, hostility, heartbreak, and other circumstances, begin to change and you regain your inner power.

In the quest to manifest our desires, we often demand that the world and all the people and things in it be different from what they presently are. We want things to change to suit our idea of order and perfection, so we try to "fix" the world and control others to accomplish it. This constitutes resistance to the flow of life, and, in the end, we suffer individually and collectively.

This doesn't mean we cannot change things, but we cannot change them if we are living in a state of resistance. In order to change something we don't like, we must first remind ourselves that whatever is happening in the moment is "just the way it is" until we personalize it and label it. We are the one who gets to decide what we're going to call the situation: good or bad, fair or unfair, etc.

The truth behind any negative situation is that there's virtually an infinite supply of everything you need to turn it around. There's always enough money, customers, time, love, friends, etc., and no situation can leave you without those things for very long if you give up the struggle and stop resisting it.

You absolutely do not need that "one" person, that "one" thing, or that "one" situation to be different or change in order for you to be happy and have what you want. Why? Because you can create something fresh and new! That possibility exists in every moment.

None of us wants to go through difficult and painful experiences, but in my life, the worst experiences that I've gone through have without exception eventually proved to be the greatest gifts. They were my teachers and each one contained within it the seed of something astonishingly good for me. However, I'll admit, sometimes it took me a while to find it—but it was always there.

I've come to understand that resistance increases suffering and prolongs the experience. Putting energy on a "bad" experience only creates more of it. Remember, we attract *more* of whatever we focus on. The moment we realize that resistance is nothing more than our ego trying to take control is the very moment that we can actually heal it. Healing resistance is simply a matter of accepting that people and circumstances are the way they "are" for the moment and letting go of our rigid intellectual opinion about how we think they "should be."

The value of non-resistance is that it speeds up the process of Deliberate Creation and gets you to the good part much faster! This shifts your energy from what you *don't want* to what you *do want*. So, if you're struggling, take that as a sign you are going in the wrong direction.

On the other hand, if you're doing something and for the most part it seems effortless, it excites you, and you love it, you're going in the right direction. And if you continue to do that, it will keep manifesting more and more of what you want and love because you're using the Law of Attraction as it was designed to be used.

The simple truth is this: struggle will bring you more struggle. Frustration will bring you more frustration. Resistance will bring you more resistance.

On the other hand, passion will bring you more passion. Joy will bring you more joy. And love will bring more love. Use this knowledge to your advantage!

Chapter 5

LIVING THE
MAGIC THAT'S
RIGHT FOR YOU

W hat you're learning to do is to just be yourself, accept yourself, and live from your own wisdom. The sooner you let go of who you think you're supposed to be and what you think you're supposed to do, the sooner you're going to become more of who you actually are, even if others are not comfortable with it.

This is why I have so much respect for the LGBTQI community when they "come out of the closet." However, coming out of the closet is not just for the LGBTQI community. It's for all of us. Most of us are hiding in the closet of *not being who we are*. "Coming out" simply means living a way that's right for you.

Albert Einstein is commonly credited with saying, "Everybody is a genius. But if you judge a fish by its ability to climb a tree, it will live its whole life believing that it's stupid."

The reality is that a fish does not have the equipment to climb trees, even if everyone tells the fish that it *should* climb trees. In other words, a fish that thinks it has to climb trees is in an automatic disconnect between its True Nature and reality. So, in the end, it will always believe that something is wrong with it, or it's stupid, or whatever—and happiness will elude him or her forever.

If you're a fish and you look around you and you see the other fish trying to climb a tree, you need to remind yourself *that's not who you are*. A fish is always going to be a fish. Climbing the tree is a choice.

If we're a fish and we spend all of our time trying to climb trees, wouldn't it be lot easier to find the nearest lake, or better yet an ocean, and start swimming? That's all you have to do. That's your True Nature.

When you're living from your True Nature and being yourself, you can be sure some people are not going to like it. No matter what you do, people will disagree with it because they're coming from a different perspective. However, it's okay if other people, including your family or your friends, don't see things the way you see them.

For example, your parents might not be able to understand how doing what you love-doing what comes natural to you and what you are truly passionate about—can support you. From their viewpoint, you have to go to school and get a secure job even if it's not your passion because security comes first. This is because they have a limited perspective. That's how they were raised, and that's their life experience.

Ultimately, when they tell you they want you to do something a certain way, it's because they want to see you happy and successful. They want you to be able to support yourself, but they only know a limited amount of ways to do that.

So, when you start talking about doing what you love, they're worried that you won't be able to support yourself, because they can't see it any other way. But just remember that they are saying those things because they want you to be happy.

Often in life, when we see the things we don't prefer, it serves the purpose of letting us know what we do prefer. This is also true of our relationship with our parents or our grandparents. We see our parents or even our grandparents struggle to make a living or making their living at something they don't enjoy. That serves a purpose in showing us that while it's important to make a *living*, what's more important is to make a *life*. **Living Your Magic is about making a life**. We make a life when we follow the path of our preferences.

In the beginning, when you follow the path of your preferences, it may not be clear to you how it's all going to unfold, but that's the way it's supposed to work. Life is supposed to unfold for you moment-by-moment. You cannot know the future. No matter how much you try to prepare for it, there are too many variables that you have no control over, especially in the world we're living in now, so the only thing you can really do is enjoy the journey. That way, no matter how things work out, you still can have a happy and fulfilling life along the way.

Keep in mind that when people try and stop you, for the most part, it's not because they're trying to destroy your dreams. It's because their world view is different than yours. That's their reality. So, don't focus on trying to convince or persuade your family, your friends, or other people that you know what you're doing. Instead, trust the innate wisdom of your Authentic Self. If you follow that, the rest will unfold for you perfectly. I promise you. But you have to believe in yourself.

Your Authentic Self, your Essence, your Soul, or whatever you choose to call it will never give up on you, even if you give up on yourself. It's always trying to lead you in the right direction and on the path of least resistance. It is working 24/7 to help you to live your highest *joy*, your *passion*, your *creativity*, and your *excitement*.

There's Nothing to "Figure Out"

We spend so much of our lives trying to figure things out. We keep wondering and asking ourselves, "What am I supposed to do next?" or "I'm not sure what I need to do next."

The reason it's so frustrating and confusing is that you're not designed to try to figure out what to do next. That's a burden. That's what the deeper wisdom and intuition of your Authentic Self is for. When you understand how to use it, you're going to alleviate that burden and you're always going to know how to steer yourself in the right direction. You'll also know if you're going in the right direction or the wrong direction in your relationships with other people.

Often when we want an insight, a solution, or a breakthrough on something, we try to figure it out using our intellect or our conditioned personal mind. We say to ourselves, "What am I going to do about this? What am I going to do about that?"

It's usually a spinning in our head (our circular thinking) and it is often filled with adrenaline.

Usually, at some point, we either get exhausted or we give up. Or, if we're not getting anywhere, we kind of throw our hands in the air and say something like, "I don't want anything to do with this anymore. I've have had enough." And, of course, what happens is because we let go of it, we drop back into the deeper mind and Intelligence behind life, and eventually we get a new insight about it and we know what to do. Sometimes it may not come immediately, but it will always show up. And into that space flows new thinking. And whenever we have new thinking, that's when our life begins to change.

Letting Go of the Illusion of Control

Like many people, I spent a lot of time being stressed about what was going on in my life and what I was going to do next. I thought it was my job to somehow take control of everything. And then as I began to have a clearer understanding of how life works, as opposed to how I thought it worked, it dawned on me that it wasn't my job to try to make everything work out or force the outcome. And if I would just get out of my own way, things would always work out. Whatever it was that got me this far was probably going to be able to take me the rest of the way. And when I came to that realization, life became much easier.

This is the way we're all naturally designed to live, but when it looks like it's all on us, we're going to feel pressure and stress. When we see that it isn't, we can let it go.

I used to think I could take control of my life by using my intellect and personal mind to run the show. However, what I came to realize is that if I do that, I'm putting all my money on my intellect or my ego to run my life. Bad decision!

I didn't know there was another choice, which was to rely on the underlying Intelligence and wisdom of my Authentic Self, this underlying guidance system that would actually fly the plane if I just stopped trying to grab the controls. And not only would it fly the plane, but it would fly it to places that were even better than the ones I was trying fly it to. And the more I saw that, the less sense it made for me to hold on to the controls.

And even though it might seem like a bumpy ride for a while, the truth is that we're not in control anyway! Not like we think we are. Life is going to do what it does. So, we can choose to enjoy the ride, make the most of it, and do great things along the way, or we can fight it, resist it, or think it should be going somewhere else.

We can complain, feel sorry for ourselves, and get caught up in what's happening in the moment, or we can just step back and get out of our own way. If we see that we don't have to steer everything "just right" or it's all going to come crashing down, we can relax. If we don't see that, we will get caught up in a toxic trance and only be able to operate at a fraction of our capacity.

So, we don't have the control we think we have anyway. And the best part is, we don't need to control anything. As you allow yourself to be guided by the inner wisdom of your Authentic Self and you stop living from your intellect and the perceptions, beliefs, and opinions of other people, there's nothing to figure out or try to control.

Living with Failure and Mistakes

Failure and mistakes are part of life. No matter what you do, there will still be times when things will not work out the way you hoped for. There's always a reason why things don't work out. Usually it's to help us to see the contrast between where we are and where we want to be. It sometimes reminds us that we're going in the *wrong direction* and we need to step back and allow our inner guidance system to self-correct.

Most of us have been conditioned since childhood to avoid failure and not make mistakes. Since it's impossible to learn anything new without making dozens or even hundreds of mistakes, depending on the complexity of what we want to achieve, the easiest way to avoid failure or not make mistakes is not to attempt to do something. And even if we do attempt it, we attempt it so tentatively that it's obvious to everyone around us that we weren't really committed so we can't be held accountable if things don't work out.

The biggest taming tool that we inadvertently faced growing up was positive and negative reinforcement. And because of our desire to be liked and rewarded for everything we do, we try to avoid the "error" part of the equation and not make mistakes.

But here's the thing. We're not supposed to know how or do what we don't know how to do. We're designed to live on a learning curve. We're natural-born learners. We were born to learn through experimentation, which involves *trial and error* as well as *trial and success*. And self-consciousness is the number one enemy of this natural kind of learning and what's possible for us to achieve in our lives. When our attention is on *how we are doing* instead of *what we are doing*, we cut off our natural learning ability at the knees.

When we were little and we were learning how to walk, we didn't learn how to walk to impress anybody. We did it because we wanted to get somewhere. It didn't matter how often we fell down. We didn't have any self-esteem issues about it or think we needed to see a therapist. We weren't saying to ourselves, "Oh God, I hope they didn't see me fall." We just made mistakes until we got it right. No big deal.

We didn't learn to talk to impress our parents or to show people how bright we were. We learned to talk to communicate with other people so they would know what we want.

Somewhere along the line, we went to school and we were taught that's not the way we are designed to learn. We were taught to keep judging ourselves along the way. So it became about us instead of about learning. As soon as it starts feeling like it's about us proving something to ourselves and others—or proving something to the world—we're screwed because then our end goal is not the task at hand but not to make mistakes or to fail.

The continual evaluation of "how am I doing" is the death of creativity because your attention is in the wrong place. Your attention is on the thinking in your head instead of what you are trying to accomplish. And when that happens, obviously you're not going to do very well. That's just common sense. This is why I keep emphasizing having *less on your mind*. Because the less you have on your mind, the more the natural learning process takes place and the more access you have to new ideas, new solutions, and new possibilities.

While all of this is going on, you're still going to make mistakes and you're still going to fail. That's part of life, but you can't let that stop you. Whatever I've achieved in my life came because I didn't stop myself from failing or making mistakes. And because I didn't stop myself, I began to succeed more and more of the time.

Here's an experiment you can play around with. Choose something that you normally wouldn't do because you feel self-consciousness. Perhaps it's asking for help on something you would like to learn or striking up a conversation with someone you don't know but would like to know. Choose anything you've been avoiding—and then just do it.

Suck at it. Fail at it. Get it wrong. But stay out of your circular, contaminated thinking the best you can. When you hear the voices of doom and gloom in your head, or you feel the feeling of impending disaster in your body, give yourself permission to fail. And you may fail at whatever it is multiple times, but if you keep going, I promise you, you will succeed more and more of the time.

See what happens. Chances are, you won't self-destruct, and you may even wind up with the assistance you need or get involved in a conversation that could change your life. Better still, you may find that the next time you get an interesting idea about what might be possible, you'll find yourself moving forward like a toddler who has no fear of failure. You'll just keep learning and making mistakes as you go forward without ever losing sight of what you want to achieve. See what happens. It might be more fun and more rewarding than you thought possible.

So, allow yourself to dare to fail. Failure is only feedback to let you know you need to go in another direction. Like a GPS, don't take it personally. If you're going in the wrong direction or you're stuck, just relax and let the deeper Intelligence of your system recalculate and then start moving in the direction you feel inspired to move. If you follow your intuition and take inspired action, eventually, you'll reach your desired outcome, or you may even end up with a much better outcome than you thought was possible.

A Past and a Future That Doesn't Exist

I'd like to begin this section by making a bold statement. And here it is: the past or the future does not exist.

Now you may say, "Okay, I agree that the future does not exist, but the past does exist."

Really? Do you actually have a past? If your answer is "Yes," then I will say the same thing to you as I say to everyone else: if your past actually exists somewhere, then take me to it or bring it to me. I'll wait! Of course, that's impossible. And that's exactly my point. The past is just illusion. It doesn't exist. What you call your "past" is nothing more than your thought-generated perception of a series of events. It's your relationship with those thoughts and memories you made up about those events.

The problem is that those thoughts and memories are *selective*. We think we have perfect, identikit, photographic memories, but we don't. In other words, you had this experience, or what you call your "past," and you try to remember it, but because memories are reconstructive by nature, you misremember things all the time.

All we really have are **selective memories** of tiny little segments of time scattered throughout the entirety of what we call our past. However, when we do this, we're not remembering what actually happened. We're remembering our *perception* or our *version* of what actually happened—and the discrepancy between the two can be massive.

The truth is, you don't have a past or a future. The past is gone, and the future is not here yet. Both are an illusion. But you say, "I remember this happening and that happened." We're not denying something "happened." What we're saying is that *after it happened,* you no longer had a past. It's gone! When it happened, it happened in that moment. Now, when you think about it, you're in another moment: this moment!

When we think of the past, what we "remember" happening is not what actually happened. Yet, we think of our memory like a video camera that recorded the event, when it's not. However, most people will argue with that. They will say, "No, it definitely happened like that."

When you look at the research in memory from people like Elizabeth Loftus (an expert in eyewitness memory), she's demonstrated how easy and effortless it is to implant false memories in people. You can find her TED talk on YouTube.

As a magician, I have also learned to create false memory in people for the purpose of entertainment. When a magician does a magic trick, he or she deliberately uses the fact that we don't remember what we think we remember. They use their skills to manipulate how people reconstruct things that just happened a few seconds ago—let alone a few weeks, months, or years ago.

A magician manipulates your perception. Let me give you an example.

I hand a deck of cards to an individual and say, "Please shuffle these cards". When they're done, I take the cards and spread them out so they can see the cards are fully shuffled. Then I hand the deck back to them and ask them to put it on the table and say, "When I snap my fingers, I want you to cut the deck you just shuffled anywhere you want." They do that and I say, "Okay we'll come back to that in a moment."

The cut deck is sitting on the table. Then I say, "We're going to do a little experiment. I am going to turn away and I want you to look at the card you cut to. Got it? Memorize that card and put it back in the deck and shuffle the deck again because I don't want to touch them."

Then I say to them, "Now let's review."

"First, you shuffled those cards. Correct?"

"Yes."

"Then I asked you to cut the cards anywhere you like? Correct?"

"Yes."

"Then I turned away and asked you to look at the card you cut to and memorize it. Correct?"

"Yes."

"Then I asked you to put the card back in the deck and shuffle the deck again. Correct?"

"Yes"

"You made all the decisions and did everything yourself. I didn't touch the cards and I did not influence you in any way. Correct?"

"Yes."

"Look at me. Think of your card. Picture it in your mind. Now make it bigger. I can see it clearly now. The card you cut to was the three of diamonds. Is that correct?"

"Yes!"

They're complexly amazed!

How is that possible when they did the entire trick themselves?

Let's look at what *really* happened.

There is a saying that describes how magic works. It goes like this …

You see what you don't see.
You don't see what you do see.
But you always see what you think you see.

What really happened is that the spectator shuffled the cards and then they handed the deck to me for a few seconds. I spread out the deck so they could see the deck was completely shuffled. But when I gave the deck back to them and asked them to cut to any card in the deck, I already knew which card they would cut to. Yet, it looked like a free choice.

Let's go back to my exact wording: "You shuffled the cards. You cut the cards anywhere you wanted to. You did all the work. You made all the decisions and did everything yourself. **I didn't touch the cards**, and I did not influence you in any way."

While most of this is true, what I am doing is *omitting from their memory* the fact that I fiddled with the cards for a few seconds. So, in the summary, I do this hand gesture by waving my hands in the air with my palms open that says, "I never touched the cards," and they go, "Yes," because all the time I am emphasizing: *you* shuffled the cards, *you* cut the cards anywhere you wanted to, *you* did all the work, *you* made all the decisions and did everything yourself.

All I did was assist them in *reconstructing a false memory* where I never touched the cards, but the truth is that I did touch the cards, but nobody ever remembers it. Not one time in the hundreds of times I have done this has anyone caught me on it.

In other words, I implanted a false memory that I never touched the cards and the person would swear that everything happened exactly as I said. They're so involved in doing the trick by themselves that the false memory I implanted that I never touched the cards is true for them!

But the truth is that after they shuffled the deck, I took it back and for few seconds the deck was in my hands. And as I handed the deck back to them, I did something almost invisible, but they never remember this because it really looks like everything happened in their hands and I never touch the deck. There are other elements to this trick such as how I knew what card they were going to cut to, but I won't reveal that here.

My point is this: how we remember something is not always how it was. It's simply how we think it was. So, our memories of the past are simply how we think they were now, in this moment.

Let's go back to our original premise that the past and the future do not exist. The only thing that really exists is how we are interacting with either of them now, in this moment. That's it! The past, present, and future can only be comprehended in this moment of thought. They don't exist anywhere else. We're making everything up based on our perception of the past or the future *in this moment.*

If you understand how your mind perceives and makes up the past, you can use this to you advantage, because in order to suffer what has happened in the past, you have to remember your version or your perception of the past *now* in this moment to create that feeling. You can only create the joy, the happiness, the sadness, or the pain of the past now, in this moment.

The same applies to the future. In order to have anxiety about the future or worry about what might happen, you have to create the future and engineer the feelings of fear, doubt, and worry now, in this moment. The joy, the happiness, the sadness, or the pain does not live in some future place waiting for you to catch it like the flu. You have to create it now, in this moment.

So, in order to suffer or grieve about your past, you have to bringing up those unhappy, scared, sad, or worried memories now, in this moment. If you want to worry about the future, you have to literally make up those thoughts in this moment in order to make yourself feel unhappy, scared, sad, or worried. But remember one crucial thing: you can only do both now, in this moment. They do not exist anywhere within you until you fabricate or re-fabricate them now.

I'm human just like everyone else. I know that's hard to believe, but occasionally I still find myself fabricating the past and the future. But now that I'm onto it, it doesn't take a hold of me anymore. I just wake up to the fact that my thoughts about the past or the future are just like a movie screen in a theatre. They're just a projection of my mind.

When you really understand that your thoughts are just a projection of your mind, the negative feelings about your past or the worrisome thoughts about the future will have very little power over you *because you know you are making them up in this moment*. And if that's true—and it is—you can make up something else!

It works like this. What we call our past is just a thought, but traditional psychology identifies it as more than a thought. They see the past as a thing. But what you'll discover is that since the past doesn't exist, it is not some "thing" that we have to get over.

This is why I don't agree with therapeutic approaches that are designed to take you into your past or talk about your past and relive the trauma to solve your problem. They're going in the wrong direction. That's like trying to get out of a hole by digging deeper.

When you go into the past, you're trying to resolve what has already been created, but the problem is that *while you're trying to do that*, your new reality is being created in this moment! This is the only thing you truly have control over.

Thinking about and analysing your past will not change the present. If you've been traumatized by some terrible event in the past, how is bringing it up again going to find a resolution? For example, if someone has been molested or abused in the past, it makes no sense to take them though it again because when you talk about or think about those events, they are happening again in your mind!

Your subconscious cannot tell the difference between a real experience from your past or an imaginary experience you're having now about that past, so it just keeps getting reinforced. This can easily be demonstrated using hypnosis by creating an imaginary experience (even a pleasant experience) and having someone experience it as though it was "real" or happening to them right now. The feelings will be *exactly the same* even though the experience is not real.

Rather than taking a person into their past or talking about their trauma, I would rather show a person how they're creating their **new reality** in this moment so they can let the past go and create something new.

I also want to make it clear that I am not knocking therapists who choose to take their clients or patients into their past. That's the way they were trained. That's what psychological studies have shown to work. However, the thing about any study is that it's only reliable if you study the right subject.

In other words, if we did a study on which type of therapy was best, if I hit you over the head with a wooden stick or a rock to resolve your issue and we decided on the wooden stick, how's that going to help? The problem is that we're studying the *wrong thing* and asking the *wrong question* and coming to a conclusion. Even if we come to the conclusion that the wooden stick is better, the fact is that neither one is necessary.

Many people are still being hit with psychological wooden sticks because studies, researchers, and therapists have decided that going into the past is part of the solution. I'm not saying it won't work. It can and it will, but it won't resolve the issue in the long-term. Those thoughts will keep coming up again and again for one simple reason: *the problem of how thought is created moment-to-moment has not been addressed.*

From my perspective, showing people that all of our feelings and emotions (by default) are created through our thought in the moment and dealing with the mechanism of how that's happening becomes a better alternative. No rock or stick needed!

If you or someone you know is dealing with a traumatic past, the good news is this: it's in the past, which no longer exists! The only way to relive the trauma is to immerse yourself in those traumatic feelings by engaging in them *in this moment*. That's really the only way you can feel bad about any event or experience. There is no other way it holds its power over you. When you relive the past, it can only come alive again in the thinking you have now, in this moment.

Why is this so important? Because the moods you feel from any thoughts, whether they are positive or negative, high or low, affect the decisions you make in that moment. In other words, the decisions you make will always be different based on your mood in that particular moment.

A lot of people act as though their feelings in the moment are telling them something about the world "out there" or are telling them something about their past or another person, but that can never be true. How you feel in the moment is dictated by how much you decide to engage in a particular thought you're having in that moment. If you don't engage or "buy into" the thought, then, by design, it cannot affect you emotionally one way or the other.

As soon as you believe that thoughts arising in your mind can harm you, or are coming from outside of you, they will affect your life and your physical world. That's when the panic and anxiety arise. That's when depression kicks in. That's when you feel the effects of PTSD. You think the thoughts you have about your past, present, or future have their own independent power and are affecting you in the moment, but they have no power unless you give them power. The effect they have on you does not start until you engage in them and give them power. And then it's downhill after that until another thought comes along.

Knowing this to be true has changed the way I live my life. I realize that it may be counterintuitive to what you've been taught, but I invite you to see how it works in your life. When you have a thought, remind yourself it's just a thought you're focusing on in that moment and invite yourself to

Chapter 6

WAKING UP
FROM THE DREAM

Your thoughts are not real, nor do they have any power over you until you decide to give them power. When you come to understand that every thought you have is *made up*, they cannot affect your life. When you hold onto a thought and you think it is real or it is telling you something about yourself, your past, or your future, it will take control of your mind and your life.

It's like being in a dream. A dream can seem so real that it's easy to mistake it for reality. We've all had the experience of waking up from a dream that seemed so real that we thought it had actually happened and then felt a sense of relief as the dream gave way to reality.

Our dreams, our illusions, and our misunderstanding about how life works will always look real. And when they do, you'll get fooled once again and fall back into the dream. But when you're awake and you know the dream is not real, you'll wake up to the fact that all that's really happening is you're getting caught up in your thinking. And when you do, everything will start to look different, including what you've been dreaming about.

When you experience your scary, negative, self-defeating, self-limiting thoughts, you are in a dream state—and this is when those thoughts have all the power. The problem is that we get so deep into the dream of our own thinking that it consumes us like a nightmare, and we think we don't have control anymore. But here's the thing: you are the person who chooses to give your thoughts power and control because *you're the person who chooses to go into the dream.*

We all have a way to wake up from our dreams so they cannot harm us, and it's simply this: when we have a thought about anything, we need to remind ourselves that a thought has no power or meaning unless we choose to believe it and act on it.

For example, I could have the thought "I think I'll kill myself today" and do nothing about it, because I'm not giving it any power or meaning. The thought "I think I'll kill myself today" has no power or meaning when it shows up. It's just a thought—nothing more and nothing less.

Another person can have the exact same thought and think it has its own independent power and they should act on it. So, we have two people thinking the exact same thought. One acts on it and the other doesn't. What's the difference? The difference is the power and meaning we give to our thoughts.

All thoughts are the same. The thought "I think I'll kill myself today" is no different than the thought "I think I'll make a cup of coffee." It's a **neutral thought** when it shows up until I decide it's important to me and I want to pay attention to it. If I pay attention to it and act on it, I'll make a cup of coffee. If not, I'll just let the thought pass through and do nothing about it. The important point here is that neither thought has any meaning or power when it shows up. We have to *add* meaning and power to the thought in order for it to affect how we feel in the moment.

When we give power and meaning to a thought, it creates emotion. For example, you remember something that is less than positive. Then you give it your attention and it starts looping in your head, so you start to remember it and think about it and it creates an emotion and you start to feel that way again.

How do we know our emotions come after the thought and they're not one and the same thing? Simple. In hypnosis, I will tell a client to take an emotional memory they have about any event in their life and tell me what actually happened without putting any emotion into it. Just tell me as an **observer**. When they do, they're amazed. They can talk about it and describe it without any emotion at all. That's when they realize how many layers of meaning they have placed on the event. When the memory shows up, they layer all this depth of emotion and perception and it makes the event become even more upsetting and traumatic than it actually was.

At this point, you may be saying, "You're not giving relevance to the event. Some events are much more traumatic than others."

No, I'm saying when you give relevance to your thinking *about the event,* you'll never let it go because you cannot see the event for what it is and put it in perspective. Your thinking about the event and playing it over and over in your head just keeps giving it more and more meaning and more and more power.

But the important point is that when the thought of the event shows up in our mind, *there is no emotion.* It's just a thought about the event, whether it's our past, another situation, or another person. As soon as the thought or memory shows up and we add *the meaning we've attached to it,* that's when we feel the emotion.

But here's the thing: There's no possible way that we can stop thoughts from coming up in our head. They're going to show up whether we like it or not. Nobody really knows exactly where they come from, but they come and go with a remarkable pace and randomness that makes hacking the details of our thoughts virtually impossible.

We all have the same amount of thoughts per day, which according to the latest university studies from the laboratory of neuro-imaging at the University of Southern California, is estimated to be around 50,000 thoughts per day. If we gave our attention to all of those thoughts, they would fry our brain, so *we selectively choose what thoughts we want to give our attention to*. And when we do, those thoughts will seem "real" or "true" for us.

Here is what I have come to realize. When I give thought number 45,967 more importance than thought number 32,542, and I selectively focus on that one thought, it becomes my reality.

Knowing how this works has given me greater understanding and peace of mind than any psychological or self-development training or practice I've ever experienced because I know that if I'm stuck in my thinking, I can remind myself I'm just stuck on *one thought out of the 50,000 thoughts* that are going to pass through me each and every day.

By making myself aware of this, the thought automatically loses its power, because I see it for what it is. *It's just one thought out of 50,000* and I don't have to believe it or buy into it. I can just let it pass through and, right behind it, I'll have another thought. And If I don't like that thought, I can just let it pass too and another one will show up. I just focus on the ones that serve me and let the others pass through.

Psychology and personal development books and programs talk a lot about controlling your thoughts. From my perspective, it is not about controlling your thoughts or even thinking positive thoughts. It's about realizing that **you are the thinker!** When you realize that you are the thinker and you are the one making up those thoughts, it allows you to be more of an **observer** than a **reactor** to your thoughts without becoming attached to them. It allows you to experience a more neutral stance of seeing without judging or believing. It will also help you to do the same in your interactions with other people.

When we come to realize more deeply that we are the thinker and our thinking is creating our experience of life moment-to-moment, we can let go of most of our thinking. Being aware that we are the thinker puts us in the driver's seat, driving where we choose to go rather than being in the passenger's seat, going where we're driven by our thoughts.

Think about this! Isn't it nice to know you don't have to put your emphasis on one particular thought because another thought is going to show up right behind it? So, what's the point of worrying about or obsessing over that particular thought? It's not going to last that long anyway—unless you choose to make it last.

So, no matter what you're going through, whether it is anger, sadness, hurt, frustration, guilt, worry, anxiety, or depression, *you're always just one thought away* from letting it go and allowing a new thought to take its place. At any moment in your life, you're only one thought away from happiness or sadness. It's *always* just one thought away!

In other words, your thoughts do not and cannot have any power over you without your permission. And the best part is that you don't have to do anything about it! You don't have to change your thoughts, stop them, fake it, remove them, or replace them. You just realize that you've suckered yourself into one particular thought and if you decide to let it go, you get a fresh start each and every moment!

Waking Up from Our Toxic Trances

We've been taught that we need to think and overthink almost everything. But the only way we will ever remove the negative, scary, limiting, or disturbing thoughts from our life is to wake up from the dream and realize we're dreaming.

Let's change the word "dream" to "trance" because that's what's actually happening. Our thinking creates a trance state. When we're *inside* the trance, our thoughts will seem real to us. The "reality tunnel" that we create looks like reality, but, in fact, it's just our version of reality.

Once you are awake to the fact that you're in a toxic trance and you see the thought you bought into as just a thought and nothing more, you will automatically drop out of the trance because it will appear nonsensical and illogical. And as soon as it no longer makes sense, you will experience things differently. Once you see a thought or a belief for what it is, you no longer want it in your life. You're done with it. The very act of identifying it releases you from it.

But also know that if you decide to go back into the trance or the dream, it's all going to seem real again. When you're inside the trance, the thought or the belief you're caught up in is going to be self-validating. And if you choose not to let it go and stay in the dream or the trance, the thought will come to life. And then, in real life, you will keep having the same experience of that thought over and over again. But if you see that it's *just a thought* and *it's not serving you*, then you can choose to let it go. And when you do, it's gone for good.

When we're in a toxic trance, it often seems like the best way to cope with the sadness, the anxiety, the pain, and the frustration is to distract ourselves. To go out and play sports, watch a movie or TV, go to yoga or a meditation class, or do anything to get our mind off our thoughts. This may work temporarily, but we also know those thoughts will return again. So, what can we do?

What if you looked at all of your thoughts for what they are? What would happen if you reminded yourself: "I am caught up in this thought at the moment, but it can't harm me in any way unless I keep holding on to it and keep giving it my attention."

A good analogy for this is a drunk walking along the street trying to get your attention. The drunk comes up and starts yelling in your ear, "You're stupid. You can't do that. You should be afraid of this thing or that person. What will they think if you do this or that? What kind of person are you if you think those thoughts?" And the list goes on and on.

Now, you could stop and have a long conversation with the drunk, thinking everything he or she says is true, or you could try to convince him or her that they are wrong. Or, you can just keep walking!

You have no control over how far the drunk follows you down the street, but one thing is for sure: at some point, if you don't give the drunk your attention, he will eventually go away. Like anything else in life, it's a psychological truth that what you give attention to grows and gets bigger. What you *don't* give your attention to just falls away.

Innocently, that's what we do with our habitual thoughts. There's a habit of old thinking that kicks in and we give our attention to it and we begin to think it's true, or we argue with it, judge it, or try to stop it, and it just keeps getting bigger and bigger. But regardless of what we do, we cannot stop these thoughts.

And you know what? We don't have to!

In other words, it's okay to have any thought, even negative, scary, limiting, or disturbing thoughts. The fact is, we can't do anything about it. They're just going to show up, but because the nature of thought is transient and changes moment-to-moment, they don't last. However, *you get to decide* how long the thought will be there and how much attention, power, and meaning you want to give it as opposed to the other 49,999 thoughts you're going to have that day.

The only way your thoughts can harm you is if you give them power and make them real. When the dreamer in you realizes it's just a dream, meaning, "I am caught up in my thinking and I am making all of this up," the thoughts and dreams lose their power over you.

I spent the first part of my life trying to increase the amount of control I had over the thoughts and feelings that passed through my head on a seemingly constant basis. When I finally understood that this is unnecessary and even counterproductive, the second part of my life has been spent giving up the illusion of control in favor of the reality and freedom of just dropping any thoughts that don't serve me because I am making them up anyway!

This is why it makes no sense to me to try to help a person change their thinking. What I am actually doing is trying to help them change their thinking with more thinking. How can that possibly help? That's like telling someone the way to remove a negative, self-defeating, or scary thought from your life is by going back into the dream. But the thought isn't the problem. **The problem is being in the dream or the trance and thinking it's real**. This is where the thought is being generated. Once you wake up, the thought goes away by itself.

If someone comes to me and asks me what they should do about how their thoughts are affecting them, or the pain they're experiencing from their thoughts, the solution is always the same. I don't have to help them analyse their thinking or go into their past. I simply say, "You are caught up in a toxic trance and nothing will change as long as you *choose* to remain in the trance. When you realize you are in a self-created trance, the thought just goes away, and you will snap out of the trance. The thought loses the power you gave it. It really has no choice to disappear because, like the drunk, you have decided you don't want to give it your attention or engage with it anymore."

In other words, the real problem is when we are in the trance, we *over-elevate the importance of our thoughts* and then we're victimized by our own thinking! However, once you see a thought for what it is and don't give it your attention, a new thought will show up in its place. When it does, you can decide if you would like to keep it or let it pass through as well. You're never going to get stuck in your thinking.

Of course, there's no rule that says you *must* wake up from your current trance. If you think your trance is serving you, why would you? So the first place to go when we're looking at any trance we're in, such as a worry trance, a victim trance, a lack of confidence trance, an "I'm not good enough" trance, or even a religious, social, or political trance, is *outside of the trance* to see it for what it is.

Everything I have just shared with you is designed to assist you in going outside your trances. To be in a place that's *beyond the trance* and ask yourself these questions: "Is this way of thinking and engaging in life really serving me in getting the kind of results I would love to have in my life? Not the kind of results I think I *need*, but the kind of results *I would love to have*." And "Is this trance allowing me to live my magic, or is it holding me back?"

If you can truly say that the trances you're in are not toxic and they are serving you, then there's nothing else that needs to be done. There is nothing in the universe that says you have to change anything, but when you step out of those toxic attachment trances, reaction trances, victimization trances, worry trances, lack of confidence trances, insecurity trances, and those "I am not good enough" trances and you ask, "Is this really serving me?" and the answer is "no," then you can make a decision to let it go!

Understanding Our Primary Motivational Mechanism

Why do we stay in our toxic trances? Why do we stay stuck where we are? To find the answer, let's look a little deeper. Psychology 101 teaches that every human being has the same Primary Motivational Mechanism. This mechanism works for everyone. No exceptions—not even you! It's automatic and built into our psychological system.

In simple terms, it works like this: you will always move *towards* what you believe to be in your best interest. And you will always move *away* from what you believe is not in your best interest. In other words, everything you do has a *positive intention*, even if it's producing negative results.

If you're caught up in something that you intellectually know is not in your best interest, or you are caught up in something you don't prefer, the only reason you are staying there is because you believe it's in your best interest to stay there rather than choosing the alternative.

Your decision is based on a belief or definition you're holding onto that says, "What I don't prefer is painful and I'm not happy, but it is familiar. If I go after what I prefer to *do* or become who I prefer to *be*, it could be more painful or scary."

So based on our Primary Motivational Mechanism, the choice of staying in what you don't prefer or what you don't want is based on it being perceived as your "best interest" even if it's painful or you're unhappy. In other words, you've made the thing you prefer—the thing you want—*scarier* than what you're holding onto that you don't prefer or what you don't want.

If you actually listen to what you're saying, you would realize it's illogical and nonsensical. How can actually *doing what you prefer to do or becoming who you prefer to be* contain the element of what you believe to be painful, fearful, or scary? It doesn't make sense.

Letting go of beliefs and definitions that are out of alignment with who we are allows us to live our magic. If you're stuck in a toxic trance in which you're unable to let go and move on, one of the ways to discover why is to look at the beliefs or definitions you are holding on to.

Here are some questions that will help you to uncover the answer.

- What would I have to believe about *myself* in order to feel this way?
- What would I have to believe about *this person or this situation* in order to feel this way?
- What am I afraid will happen in this situation if I actually allowed myself to *do* what I prefer to do or *be* who I prefer to be?

Whatever answer you come up with, ask yourself this question: "Why would I assume this to be true?"

And what you'll discover is that 100 percent of the time, *you are making it up!*

The next question to ask yourself is: "What would be the worst, most terrifying thing I could imagine would happen if I actually let go of all these fearful negative beliefs and definitions?"

And whatever answer comes up for you, remind yourself, *you are making that up too!*

Once you discover or identify the beliefs or definitions that are holding you back, you don't have to change them or do anything about them because they'll immediately appear nonsensical and illogical. And when they do, you won't want them in your life anymore. When you really see a thought or a belief for what it is, *which is something you are always making up*, it's much easier to let go of it.

We forget that when we're stuck in something, we don't have to stay there. The very next thought could change everything and then we're on our way to a new experience of life. Sometimes all it takes is just one new insight to change our definition or belief of "that's the way it is."

I often see people experience rapid and immediate change because they have one new insight. Sometimes one, genuine insight can override most, if not all, of their previous experience. This helps them move beyond their theories and beliefs about how they are limited, or how something is 'too good to be true,' or about how much happiness is possible. It helps them to connect to their own inner creative wisdom and deeper Intelligence where anything is possible. That's the magic of insight.

When you're caught up in a belief or a definition that is not serving you, the "red flag" will always be *negative feelings and emotions.* When that happens, you know you are back in the toxic trance. Your state of being is out of alignment with your Authentic Self. And when you wake up to the fact that you've gone back into the trance, *just knowing that* will take you right out of it and you'll be open to a new way of looking at your reality. And once again, you'll be living your magic!

The Mental Committee

We've been talking about getting caught up in our toxic trances. I don't know about you, but when I fall into a toxic trance, it feels like I have a Committee of people in my head. And whatever's going on in my life, different people on the Committee give their opinion. One says, "Why are you feeling that way? You shouldn't be feeling that." And another says, "It's okay to feel that." Another says, "You better change your thinking." Regardless of what's happening, they always have an opinion.

I spent most of my life thinking that no matter what I was going through in the moment, one of those people on the Committee was "right" and I should listen to them. So, I would sometimes join the meeting—because they're always having a meeting—and I would weigh in with my opinion. I would argue and debate with them and have these dialogs.

Then one day it finally hit me: what if none of them knew what they were talking about? Then it occurred to me that I didn't need to have a mental advisory Committee in my head, so I decided to walk out of the meeting. And what I discovered was that without listening to the Committee, my world didn't fall apart. So, I just stopped listening to those voices, because I was making them up anyway!

The more understanding you have about the true nature of reality and how it is created, the less attention you will pay to your mental advisory Committee. You can just let the Committee keep meeting because that's what they do, but you don't have to sit in on the meeting!

And if you don't have a mental advisory Committee, something else happens. The inner creative wisdom of your expanded Authentic Self will come through and take their place. It will lead you, guide you, and help you resolve whatever you need to resolve and bring you back to innate mental health and well-being.

On the other hand, the more we don't understand the true nature of reality and how it's created, the more insecure we're going to feel. And, the more insecure we feel, the more compelling the Committee's arguments will seem.

For a long time, I didn't know you could just pay no attention to the Committee. Once again, if you don't give something your attention, it goes away. If you give a thought your attention and try to analyze it, fix it, stop it, change it, improve it, or to get it to be more positive, all of that thinking is just another voice on the Committee—even though it seems to have a more positive message.

In short, we can't *think* our way to happiness and well-being. No one can. It's impossible. All the thinking we're doing doesn't get us any closer to happiness and well-being because, in the end, all of it is just more thinking!

Now you may be saying, "Well, how do I do that? How do I not pay attention to the Committee?"

What you must understand is that question is just another Committee member's voice. But all that's really going on is that you're caught up in your thinking in the moment, nothing more. Remember, no matter how *real* a thought looks, it's just a thought.

Understanding this is what cleans up your psychology. Yet, most people keep engaging with their thoughts moment-to-moment as though they're real, not realizing we're just making everything up as we go along!

I did that for years and years and the problem was that I was getting better at looking at the *content* of my thinking—about everything—so I thought I was onto something. Essentially, I was doing something that wasn't working and getting better and better at it. Now that I understand what's really happening, I'm less interested in whether what I'm thinking about in the moment is right or wrong, good or bad, because it's all made up anyway!

What we are pointing to is the fact that we have to keep reminding ourselves that we make up our experience of life, moment-to-moment. Sometimes we like what we made up and sometimes we don't.

If we really had that much choice or control over it, I think we'd all make up beautiful experiences every single moment. But the reality is that you're going have those days when everything's going along great and suddenly you feel anxious. Or, you think you're great and then you think you're an idiot. That's simply the "dance of life." You're going to have both. But when you understand what's happening, which is that you're just caught up in your thinking in the moment, you get less affected by it.

I also thought that when I understood all of this, I wouldn't get angry, anxious, or worried, or I wouldn't get upset with people because I know where my experience is coming from. But to be honest, I *still* do it. So now I've just learned to apologize more. "I am sorry. I just got caught up in my thinking" or "I am sorry. I acted like an idiot."

Negative, scary, or unhelpful thoughts are going to come and go whether we consciously think about them or not. And we're not alone. There are seven and a half billion other people on the planet doing the same thing! They're all having different experiences based on their thinking in the moment.

No matter who we are or where we are, when we listen to the Committee in our head, we're going to get into trouble. For many years I didn't know I had a choice whether or not to listen to the Committee. I thought when a Committee member's voice spoke, I had to listen. I didn't know that most people, especially people with anxiety and depression, don't know they have a *choice* whether or not to listen to what goes on in their head.

I used to listen to the Committee member with the loudest voice, not knowing there was a choice. And sometimes I still find myself listening, but not for very long because I'm on to it. I know what's going on. And now you do. But remember this: the more interested you are in the Committee in your head, the more you will listen to it.

Some people think, "What's going to be there if I let go of the Committee?"

The fact is, the Committee is only there when you're giving it your attention. Where's your Committee when you're not worrying? Where does your lack of confidence go when you're not thinking about feeling unconfident? Where does your insecurity go when you're not thinking about insecurity? It's just not there when we don't give it our attention.

I used to think that worry, lack of confidence, anxiety, depression, or insecurity was stored somewhere inside of me waiting to jump out and get me. But that's not true. All that is really happening is people getting caught up in their thinking in the moment and making stuff up as they go along.

The important point here is that you don't need a Committee. The inner wisdom of your Authentic Self will always give you what you need in the moment when you have less and less on your mind.

As you really begin to understand and get a feel for this, you'll learn to trust yourself more and more, instead of listening to the Committee in your head.

Chapter 7

IT'S IMPOSSIBLE TO CREATE A FUTURE BASED ON THE PAST

I t never ceases to amaze me how many people try to create their future based on their past. If you think about it, on what planet would that ever work? Even when you make an investment, the company you are investing in is obligated to tell you in writing: "Past performance is not a predictor of future results."

If we didn't live in a thought-created world that's happening moment-to-moment, looking to create the future based on the past might have some logic. However, because we live in a thought-created world and the nature of thought is *transient* and *changes moment-to-moment*, we can't predict the future based on the past, because that doesn't take into account any *new thoughts* we might have when that future moment shows up.

Also, when the future arrives, we will be a different person than we are in this moment because we're constantly changing moment-to-moment. The future will always be an incomplete equation because we can never really take into account what we will be like or what we will be thinking in any particular future moment. So, there's no way to know how we'll be feeling in that moment when the future becomes the present.

The idea that we "just know" we'll be devastated if such and such happens is the result of looking into our *already-created past*, not towards the *not-yet-created future*. We don't know what new possibilities for action or change will occur to us in any given moment. So, the idea that we "already know" how the future will take form (let alone how we'll react to it) is naïve at best and self-fulfilling at worst.

The way it works is that we tend to think of the future as a logical extension of the past and the present. So, we look to our memory and our imagination to create a baseline idea of what we think will happen in the future. Then we find ourselves either dreading it or chasing after the excitement of what we have convinced ourselves will be coming our way. Yet, the missing piece is still the thoughts that will occur to us in the moment that future shows up. This is what creates both the positive expectation or the fear of our imagined future and our actual experience of that "future" when it shows up.

In other words, every element we perceive about our imagined future is a product of our thinking in this moment. That would be great if everything worked out exactly as we imagined, but the variables are far more arbitrary than we think.

That's why the more we think about a future event, the more we either vacillate between hope and fear, or we lock ourselves into positive expectation. Our fixed prediction of future events and our reaction to and the experience of those events is what we proceed to sell ourselves and everybody around us on and defend at all costs. And we haven't even gotten to the most important part yet.

When the future actually arrives, our experience of it will be made up of the sum total of—you guessed it—whatever thinking we have in that moment. And since there's no way to accurately predict what thinking will occur to us in that moment, there's no way to accurately predict the future.

Simply put, we're all terrible at predicating the future.

This brings us to two inescapable conclusions.

1) Toxic "Worry Trances" Make No Sense

All worry is based on future events. My experience with people who are chronic worriers is that they believe that the act of repeatedly thinking scary or unsettling thoughts about the future will either keep them safe, spur them into action, or both. They are "buying into" the illusory "worry trance" that says: "If I worry, it will somehow help the situation or change something."

When you're in a toxic worry trance, it will seem like a valid response. It will make sense like all trances make sense to us. If the trance says, "If I don't worry that will be a bad thing because worrying is a good thing" or "If I worry it means I care," then you will continue to worry. But, once again, I need to remind you that whatever trance you are in is the way the world will *look to you*, not *the way things are*.

I also I want to make another important point here concerning worry, because this is where a lot of people get stuck. When I talk about not worrying, one of the objections that often comes up is, "If I don't worry, it means I don't care, and I don't want to be a person who doesn't care."

A lot of the time people use **care** and **worry** as synonyms. They actually think worrying *is* caring! So, the idea is, "If I stop worrying, I'll stop caring," as though they're the same thing. If you think they are the same thing, it's going to seem logical to have the fear that if you don't worry, you won't care anymore. But I am going to suggest that worrying and caring are *not* the same thing.

Worrying is being in a fearful, reactive place to something. Caring is about finding out how to assist to make things better and facilitate change.

In order for me to do that, I need to show up and be grounded in my True Authentic Self, because if I really care about something or someone, what's going to be required is for me to be in my full power.

When I am in my full power and not fearful, I can consider what needs to happen in this situation and what seems to be good for me and everyone else involved. This allows me to show up and engage in making that happen. That's *real caring*.

The difference is that you're coming from a place of not worrying and not fearing instead of a not caring. So, when I talk about not worrying, people often confuse it to mean, "I wouldn't be a caring person" or "I wouldn't be caring about myself." What they're missing is that worry and caring are not the same thing!

The idea is to go *beyond worry* and connect at a deeper level to free yourself to be everything you are *beyond that worry* so that you can access more of your resources to help yourself and others. Rather than living in a reactive, fearful way about what might happen, it's knowing that when you go into a worry trance, it's not serving you in any way.

Worry is always tied to some future event. Yet, no matter how much we worry about the future, it will be what it is. I have an ongoing bet I offer to people, and it's simply this: "I will bet you $1,000 that you cannot tell me one instance in your life where you worried about the future and your worrying changed the outcome."

No one has ever made this bet with me because they know they will lose. But the strange thing is, **we keep doing it**! We keep "betting" that we can somehow influence the future by worrying about it. How ridiculous is that?

Every worry you have—every single one of them—is based on a false assumption that what you are worrying about is an accurate prediction of a likely future. Yet, when we see that all worry, *without exception*, is unconnected in any way to what will actually happen in the future, it becomes illogical and easier to let go of when it arises.

We may still worry from time to time, but we're less likely to give worry the power of the "predictor" of future events. The unquestionable reality is that when we drop into a toxic worry trance, it obscures our innate Intelligence and wisdom, it overrides our common sense, and, if we keep doing it, over time, it can even affect our health. So, the first inescapable conclusion about our future is Toxic "Worry Trances" Make No Sense.

2) Our New *Future* Reality is Being Created in *this Moment*

The truth is that I can only imagine my future based on my current thinking in this moment. However, if I know my Authentic Higher Self is constantly downloading wisdom from deeper Intelligence moment-to-moment, I also know that I don't need to imagine my future. When my future gets here and becomes the present moment, the wisdom of my Authentic Self will inform me, and something will occur to me that will be useful in that moment— exactly when I need it most. In other words, I will know *what* to do *when* I need to know it, so why waste a moment worrying about what might happen in the future? That's all taken care of when I get there!

I've come to see that my new reality or my future reality is being created in this moment. When I get out of my own way and have *less on my mind* and I rely on the capacity of the inner creative wisdom of my Authentic Self to prompt me on what I need to know and do and when I need to know and do it, I worry less and less about the future. And on those occasions when I fall into the trance of my future that I'm conjuring up in my current imagination, I'm on to it, so I can relax. I'm less thrown by sudden shifts in my circumstances or in my thinking in the moment.

Another important point to remember is that what has happened to us in the past or what we think is going to happen to us in the future has absolutely no correlation with *how we feel in this moment*. Why? Because reality can only be created in the present moment. It's our *thoughts in the moment* that are creating our reality. So, what happened in the past or what we think might happen in the future cannot affect how we feel in this moment until we add *meaning* to it. This is what causes us to feel the way we do in this moment.

It works like this. We are all "meaning-makers." Nothing has built-in meaning. We attach meaning to everything. I know this may sound like an odd statement, but it's true. Life is meaningless. There is no automatic, built-in meaning to anything. If you want to put it another way, you can say the meaning of life is the meaning you give to it moment-to-moment.

The meaning you give it ultimately determines what you get out of it. When you understand you are the "meaning-maker," you'll no longer be run by your past or your imaginary future. You'll start to live in the moment more insightfully and less reactively.

The one constant we all share is that our thoughts about ourselves and the world are always changing. The fact is, we cannot hold a thought in our head for very long. It's interesting that we don't know what we'll be thinking in five minutes, five hours, five days, or five years from now, yet we're still pretty convinced we know what our future is going to look like. And, of course, we'll be wrong because we cannot predict what our thoughts and our life will be like when our future shows up, so why not let it go and just live in the moment? Because this is where our new reality is being created.

So whatever models we have for predicting the future are only accurate to the extent that there are no variables. In other words, they are only accurate if we will be same person we are today, and our thinking never changes. But that's not going to happen. We're constantly changing and the variables will continue to change without our permission. Life is going to do what it does, and we have no control over it. More importantly, we don't need to have control over it because we can respond to it in 'real time' moment-to-moment.

When you see this truth is when you start to live your magic. And as you keep seeing it more and more and have more understanding, new opportunities, new solutions, and new possibilities will come your way. You'll be able to use this understanding to help yourself and to help others. And as you continue to do that, your world and their world will begin to change.

Looking to the Unknown

There's another possibility for looking at your future and it's much more exciting. And that is to look to the **unknown**. To look to what has "not yet been created." Because everything we want to change in our world and in our life must come from the unknown, not the known.

If we try to create from the known, essentially, we're trying to create from our past. However, what if you could live in uncertainty or live in the unknown in a way that allowed for something new to come in? Not necessarily a resolution to your problem or situation, but something *entirely new*. What would it really be like to live in the unknown and stop trying to fix the known? To go into the unknown and see what's there. To open yourself up to something new and to allow yourself to be completely wrong about everything you think must happen or how you think things should turn out.

Every creative breakthrough (and there is a lot of research on this) involves a compete break from the previous train of thought. Creativity is not *evolutionary*, it's *revolutionary* because it comes from a new thought. All creative ways and inspiration come when the old way of thinking is interrupted.

All new, innovative ideas and solutions come from the unknown—the not yet created. The known is comprised of what you've already thought, including your beliefs and habitual ways of thinking about yourself, your life, and your world. The unknown is the source of all new ideas and new possibilities.

The problem is that when people are trying to find a new solution or a new way to live their life, they tend to look *backwards* to what they already know, but the answer to what we need in the moment cannot be found in the past or what we already know. Trying to live this way is like trying to drive your car forward while looking though the rearview mirror. Sooner or later, usually sooner, you will crash.

I often work with people who have had some degree of success in the past, but now they are stuck because they're trying to do the same thing they did in the past and it is not working. That's because what worked in the past *may not* and *probably will not* work in the present or the future. What we want are new ideas and new creative solutions. In order to have this, we must embrace the unknown to find what we're looking for.

Our thinking in the moment is both the bridge to the past that keeps us stuck in our old thinking and a bridge to the present and the future that carries us to freedom. So, we only have two choices. We can either stand on the bridge and look back at the known, the world we've been in and have already created, or we can turn around and look towards the unknown, the world of possibility.

So, your choices are to look back at the world you've been in and see how it was already created and try to create from that, or you can turn around and look towards the unknown. You can turn around and look at the **now**, because the now and the unknown are the same. You cannot be in the now if you're thinking about the known because the known is in the past.

The unknown is the place where everything new comes from. When we enter the unknown, we're at the end of our habitual thinking. When we turn and face the unknown, what we're really doing is embracing the inner creative wisdom within us. And when we embrace that, we enter into a new world. We get an opportunity to stand in the unknown and be close to our Authentic Self.

What I see is when people understand this, they get excited and talk about new ideas and new opportunities. Then they usually say, "I totally agree this is the best way to create my future, but how am I going to apply this to where I am right now?"

What they fail to see at first is that *you can't*, because where you're at right now is based on your old thinking. With new thinking, you can't go back to that old world and try to fix it. That's called the "Donald Trump Syndrome!"

You have to create a new world or a new life for yourself, but if you try to fix the old world or fix your old life, nothing is going to change. You can't live in an old, thought-created world and have a new thought at the same time. It's not possible.

When we're hypnotized by our habitual thinking and looking at the past for answers, it can make it seem like stepping into the unknown is dangerous and risky. But it really isn't. It can be a little scary at first because we're all used to living in the content of our previous thinking, but when we enter the unknown, we're not caught up in our previous thinking. We're at the end of our previous thinking.

When we talk about the unknown, what we're talking about is everything forward from this moment. And even if you have a plan for the future and decide the general direction you want to take, you still have to move into the unknown.

This is what I know. When you have a lot of insecure thoughts about entering the unknown, you will get into overthinking about it. When this happens, you're trusting your ego, your intellect, and your conditioned personal mind. You're not trusting the inner creative wisdom of your Authentic Self. However, when you're not run by your intellect, your ego, and your conditioned personal mind, your thinking settles down and you automatically move into the unknown. So instead of it being a scary experience, it's an enjoyable and exciting experience as you trust your inner creative wisdom to move you forward and take the next step. The magic can only happen when you look to the unknown.

The Truth about Self-Confidence

When stepping into the unknown, the subject of self-confidence often comes up. Now you would think that because I know all this stuff, I would be self-confident all the time. But the truth is that my own level of self-confidence fluctuates. Some days I feel like I can take on the world. Some days I feel like I should hide under the blanket and stay there for the rest of the day.

It doesn't bother me anymore because I understand that my feelings about whether I'm confident or not don't tell me about myself, what I want to accomplish, or what I am capable of achieving. My feelings of confidence or lack of confidence are telling me about *my thought in the moment*. And that's going to change moment-to-moment.

When it comes to stepping into the unknown, there are two factors at play that determine our self-confidence. The first is **competence**. A person who is competent has the skills and abilities necessary to do something. You wouldn't want an incompetent mechanic to work on your car or an incompetent surgeon to operate on you. Whatever you choose to accomplish will require a certain level of competence. But here's the thing: often, the only way to develop competence is by taking action from a place of *incompetence*.

Think about the activities you do effortlessly like walking, talking, or perhaps riding a bike. There was a time when you were completely incompetent in those activities, but you took action anyway and, over time, you developed a high level of competence.

So, what allowed you to take action when you knew you were incompetent and could plainly see that your skill level wasn't good enough to master the job at hand? When you recognized and accepted that you would make mistakes, fall over, and get it wrong. In other words, when you were a little child, you didn't have unshakeable self-confidence. You had no idea what was and wasn't possible for you, but you had something far more valuable: the willingness to take action, to step into the unknown, and to learn. You weren't hung up on the concept of failure. As a result, you were willing to explore, learn, evolve, and grow.

In the process, you didn't just develop skills and abilities; you also developed a deeply embodied understanding of many of the principles that govern the world you live in. Today, you use those embodied understandings automatically without even thinking about them. So, feeling competent plays an important part in our perception of self-confidence.

The second factor at play in having self-confidence is how much we are willing to **trust the wisdom and guidance of our expanded Authentic Self**. When most people talk about self-confidence or their lack of self-confidence, you'll often find that the "Self" they're referring to is the ego or the "little me." But when you listen to people who have accomplished truly extraordinary things, you often hear them refer to some 'greater intelligence' that they've tapped into. In other words, the source of insight and inspiration to accomplish what they desire always came from something greater than their "little me" or their ego—something we're referring to as our Authentic Self.

My experience is this: when a person develops competence and gets in touch and aligns with their expanded Authentic Self, they open up to a world of possibility and potential because they have a greater understanding of what they've got going for them and how life really works. And developing competence and understanding of how life works and how you create your reality moment-to-moment is where you'll find true self-confidence.

Living Your Magic Moment-to-Moment

Living your magic is a moment-to-moment experience. For me, it's just being conscious in the moment. By that I mean I'm constantly checking my *feelings*. Am I in a *good feeling* or a *bad feeling*?

Just ask yourself: "Am I feeling calm and settled, or am I feeling agitated, worried, or stressed?"

If you are, then just remind yourself: "I'm getting caught up in my thinking." And the best part is that you don't have to do anything to correct it. Just this awareness alone will kick in the deeper Intelligence and wisdom of your Authentic Self. And, if you stay out of your own way, everything will settle down and you'll find the answer or the solution that's perfect for you.

What you're learning is to be the **observer** of your thinking, rather than the **victim** of your thinking. By that I mean you just notice your thoughts without fusing with them, believing they are real, or becoming overwhelmed by them. You're still going to be deeply affected by people and events outside of you, but you know that no matter what's happening in your life, your well-being is never at risk.

When things don't seem to be going the way I want them to, or I feel agitated, worried, stressed, or doubtful, I also check to see if I am making *assumptions*. We have a tendency to make assumptions about everything. The problem with making assumptions is that we believe they are true. All the drama you have lived in your life has been rooted in making assumptions. Assumptions set us up for suffering because we only see what we want to see and only hear what we want to hear. In short, when we make assumptions, we're caught up in our own version of reality.

We're pretty good at going inside our heads and making up a bunch of stuff that isn't true. And because we're constantly feeling the *effects* of our thinking, we think it's true. When I start making assumptions about people or circumstances, I'll often remind myself, "Robert, you're full of crap right now. You're thinking the way you see this and the way you're making things up in your head right now is aligned with reality. But the fact is that you wouldn't be feeling this way if you *were* in alignment with reality." So, I look at how full of crap I am in the moment and then I let it go.

I decided that is what "enlightenment" is really about. It's being less full of crap today than I was yesterday. In other words, aligning myself with reality, not just my version of reality. This is how I measure my personal growth.

Any answers I need will always come if I get out of the way. By that I mean that when I give up my opinion of how something should be, how it ought to be, or how it needs to turn out in order for me to be happy, I open myself to fresh new ideas, new solutions, and new opportunities.

In order to know if I'm making progress, I take a look at my current ideas, insights, and solutions to see how much of it is from my personal mind and my intellect (what I already know) as opposed to the inner creative wisdom of my uncontaminated Authentic Self. I also look at how surprised I am I when I come up with new ideas, new solutions, and new possibilities because when I surprise myself and I think, "Where did *that* come from?," I know it's coming from my inner creative wisdom. It's at this point I start to look for clues to take **inspired action** that always guides me toward the best possible outcome.

So, what we're doing is introducing something new into the **flow of life** and we're seeing where it takes us. We're saying, "Let me open myself up to fresh new thinking about this and see what shows up." And when you do that, things will start to change.

All miracles involve a shift in perception. When you're open to something new, you will be amazed what new, exciting possibilities, opportunities, and synchronicity will show up in your life.

Chapter 8

YOU ARE CREATED
TO BE A CREATOR

U p until now, we've been mainly focusing on the physical and psychological aspects of living our magic. Now we're going to integrate the non-physical creative aspect so that we can use both to take advantage of the power of Deliberate Creation.

Each one of us is a Creator. In fact, we're created to be a Creator. However, before we discuss how the process of Deliberate Creation works, we need to understand a very important basic principle: we live in a **vibrational universe**. Everything is vibrating. If you look at anything that appears solid through a very large microscope, you will see that everything is composed of vibrational energy. Nothing is solid—not even you.

Thought is also vibrational energy and it's behind everything that has ever been created or ever will be created. Let's take a look at how this works.

First of all, we live on a planet of contrast. It's important that we take some time to understand the purpose and value of contrast because it's the starting point of all Deliberate Creation. Contrast is designed to help you become aware of what you *don't want*. And by seeing what you don't want, you are inspired to create what you *do want*. This causes you to launch your desire. As soon as you launch your desire, it creates a non-physical vibrational reality or a point of attraction.

As the contrast in life between what you don't want and what you do want inspires you, you have to find a way to be a vibrational match for what you desire. What this means is that you can't keep thinking about and talking about why you need something or how much you want it *because you don't have it*. You have to think of it in terms of your highest *joy*, your *passion*, and your *excitement* and then allow those things to be the driving engine of your desire.

The most challenging part of the Deliberate Creation process is staying in the emotional vibrational state that matches what you want. It's easy to feel positive, excited, and happy for a while and believe everything is coming together, but it's also easy to fall back and get caught up in your old thinking of why it's not possible or how difficult it is. And as soon as you do, you lose your point of attraction.

As you've already learned, when you realize you're caught up in your old, habitual, contaminated thinking, you don't have to change it or do anything about it. All you have to do is see it for what it is, which is nothing more than a thought you're making up in the moment, then just let it go and get back into an emotional vibrational state that feels good and matches your desire.

Here's how the process of Deliberate Creation works.

- Step 1: Through *contrast*, I learn about *what I don't want*. This points me towards *what I do want*.
- Step 2: I launch my desire for what I want.
- Step 3: I think about what I want and why I want it in terms of my highest *joy*, my *passion*, and my *excitement*.
- Step 4: I stay in the emotional vibrational state that matches it. And as long as I do that, it feels *good*. And if I get out of the

way, not only do I feel *better*, but everything will come together without any effort or struggle on my part. Any action I take will not be coming from fear or trying to force the outcome, rather it will be *inspired action* which leads me to do the right thing at the right time.

• Step 5: Finally, when I get what I want, I'm back to Step 1 and a whole new set of contrasting experiences causes me to launch a new desire. I do this for the rest of my life because this is how the process of Deliberate Creation works.

What I want you to understand is that this process is never-ending because you are always going to desire more. And what I would like to convince you of is that the joy in life is in that motion *towards your desires*. It's in letting go of resistance and letting yourself have that sweet ride of moving towards your desires.

You may think your desire is the end result, but what you're really reaching for is the glorious experience of knowing the power of your creative ability and taking the path of least resistance. Also, the experience of making it okay to have contrast in your life. Then launching your desire and even recognizing that perhaps you're not up to speed with it and then deliberately getting up to speed with it.

The most thrilling part is having the experience of witnessing everything coming together: seeing the synchronicity, seeing circumstances and events all cooperating with you. And then when it happens—and it will—you can stand in that feeling of thankfulness. You'll come to understand that you have focused your **desire** into **being** or manifestation with the power of your mind.

Entering the Vibrational Vortex of Creation

In the same way the universe or the Formless Creative Intelligence behind life is responding to the thoughts of your Physical Self, it's also responding to the thoughts of your Non-Physical Self or your Authentic Self, which causes a very powerful point of attraction toward everything you're asking for in life.

The best way to explain this is to imagine there is a vibrational field of energy or an environment where everything is created. It moves *towards* everything and *pushes against* nothing. We're going to call this the "Vibrational Vortex of Creation."

Imagine a world where billions of people are attempting to create what they desire and there's a vibrational field of energy or Vibrational Vortex that contains the *non-physical equivalent* of what they desire. An environment where there is never any doubt. An environment where there is no squabbling over resources, where there is no pushing against others, and where there's no competition. In other words, if one person receives their desire, it doesn't cut off the desires of anyone else.

I want you to step back far enough so you'll come understand that no matter how it looks to you in any moment in time, that's what's really going on.

What you, me, and the rest of humanity is asking for is already available in this non-physical Vibrational Vortex of Creation. The problem comes when we add doubt and contradiction to it, and it pushes away our desire because of the conflicting energy. This means you have to be willing to move in the direction of what you *want* and no longer continue to beat the drum of what you *don't want* or believe you cannot have.

In other words, if you're struggling with money and you continued to beat the drum of "I don't have enough money" or "It's not fair that he or she has so much money" or "The wealth is not being distributed equally and there's not enough of us getting our fair share," you will deprive yourself of the vibrational match that's necessary for you to manifest money in *your* life. Now, you could be entirely correct about all of the above, but it's still not going to help you manifest more money in *your* life.

Here's what's happening in the background. Whatever you choose to create, including the money, your desire is already in this non-physical vibrational reality and it's being held in what we might call, for lack of a better term, a "Vibrational Escrow." Nobody has access to what you want but you. Nobody can "get in there" and take your escrow.

What happens with so many people is that they stand outside the Vibrational Vortex of Creation and complain about not having what they want, but they are the only one who can get in there! Their Vibrational Escrow is in this non-physical Vibrational Vortex of Creation. Everything in life you want is in there.

When you ask for something new, your thoughts and intention are acted upon by your Authentic Higher Self which operates within this non-physical Vibrational Vortex of Creation. Everything that's necessary for the fulfilment of it is being summoned to it. All cooperative components you need are being drawn to it.

For example, when you ask for a lover—a lover of a certain nature or a lover of a common interest, a lover that's a vibrational match to you— the vibrational energy of that particular type of lover is being energetically summoned and every component you've asked for has been summoned. It's already there in that Vortex.

The question is: are *you* a cooperative component? Are you cooperative enough that you are being drawn into your own Vortex? A vortex where all your lovers are, where all your money is, where all your answers are, where all your clarity is and where all that you have vibrationally become is? Or, are you standing *outside of it*, beating the drum of: "I've been asking for this for so long and it never comes to me and I'm getting tired. All the good men (or women) are taken and it's not fair. My friend has a lover and she doesn't deserve him! She treats him like crap and they're still together! I could be such a wonderful lover, but I don't have a lover. Poor me."

Yes, you do! You've got a lover. You're just not vibrationally where your lover is! Your lover's *vibrational energy* is in the Vortex wanting to be with a person who matches your vibrational core frequency. But you have to show up! And even if you don't show up for this lover, the deeper Intelligence behind life has the ability to keep putting in a new lover if the current lover has found somebody else until you finally decide to get into vibrational alignment.

A steady stream of lovers is making its way to your Vortex on the rare occasion you might actually show up and stop complaining, stop doubting, and stop resisting. You have to want to be in that matching vibrational Vortex more than anything else! You have to want to be in there more than complaining, more than validating your excuses, more than being "right."

Often, we are so "right" about what we believe because we've got *evidence*. We've got evidence that life is working against us or we can't have what we want. And we use that evidence as our justification for not to going into the Vortex. But here's the thing: in order to be in the Vortex, we have to give up our evidence, our excuses, our justification, our complaining, and our doubting. As soon as we give all that up, we will find ourselves in this magical swirl of synchronicity where everything is working out for us easily and effortlessly.

And it starts by talking about and focusing on what you prefer, following your highest *joy*, your *passion*, and your *excitement*. Getting into the Vibrational Vortex is learning to praise rather than criticize, learning to be optimistic rather than pessimistic. It's training yourself, thought by thought, to focus on what you prefer instead of what you don't prefer.

However, in order to get into the Vibrational Vortex of Creation, you first have to accept the idea that this "vibrational reality" actually exists. Now, if you fancy yourself as a logical, left-brain thinker, this could be difficult at first. But what we're referring to is the same vibrational reality that creates worlds. This vibrational reality precedes physical reality. In other words, there is *always* a non-physical vibrational *equivalent* of something before there's a physical manifestation of it. This is what's behind all creation.

Okay, let's go back a step so you understand how everything in the universe is created. Science says that in the beginning there was nothing. So, the source of everything is nothing.

When we say nothing, we mean the "no-thing"—the Formless Creative Intelligence behind life. Every single thing that has ever been created has come from the *formless* into the *form*. It starts as a vibrational energy of asking or desire.

Look around you and behind everything you see, whether it's a new product, a new service, a new invention, a new book, a new song, a new solution to a problem, or anything else, and see that it started with a new idea. Where did this idea come from? It didn't come from our brain or our intellect because our brain and our intellect *can only create from what they already know.* In order to create something new, we have to go *beyond* what we already know. So, everything comes from nothing or the "no-thing," from the formless into form, from the non-physical to the physical. This all takes place inside the Vibrational Vortex of Creation.

Unfortunately, most people try to create *outside* this Vibrational Vortex of Creation. When that happens, they start trying to force the outcome. They put a lot of effort into accomplishing their goals, their relationships, making more money, trying to make the world a better place, and almost everything else in their lives. Most of this effort is focused on what they don't want. The majority of the effort from the majority of the people on this planet is coming from *outside* the Vibrational Vortex of Creation—and that's why life feels so difficult!

Efforting can also appear to be *positive*, but it's still efforting. For example, let's use affirmations. Most people think positive affirmations are a good idea, but that is often not the case. Let's say you are affirming more money. You go to the mailbox and don't have as much money in your bank account as the bills that are piling up. So, from your place of worry, concern, and fear, you begin using the process of positive affirmations.

The problem is that when you use positive affirmations and you're outside the Vortex of Creation, your affirmations draw your attention to what you *don't want* or *don't have*. But if you should find yourself *in* the Vortex of Creation, where just for a moment you stop focusing on what you don't want or don't have, but instead you get into a *state of Being* where you feel good and *then* say your positive affirmations, the feeling is entirely different because there is no vibrational conflict or resistance.

In other words, if you're thinking about what you want and it feels *bad* to you because you don't have it, it's not helping you to say positive affirmations because you are vibrationally out of sync. The first order of business is to get vibrationally in sync with your Authentic Higher Self by having *less on your mind* and getting into a *state of Being* where you feel *good*. This automatically puts you back in the Vibrational Vortex of Creation.

If you're outside the vibrational Vortex of Creation and you affirm, "I am the creator of my own life experience," you are not going to feel very good because the "life experience" that you've created is not what you want. But if you are in the Vibrational Vortex of Creation and you affirm, "I am the creator of my own life experience," you feel empowered. It is life-giving. You feel exhilarated because you are connecting to your highest *joy*, your *passion,* and your *excitement.*

When you're in the Vibrational Vortex of Creation, you will not only *feel* it, but you will want to be in there more often. When you're out of it, you will feel that too. When you're out of it, it's helpful to know what thoughts threw you out of it and then let those thoughts go. And then, with a clear, uncluttered mind, you are automatically back into the place of least resistance where all the resources you need are gathered and held until you vibrationally align with them through your thoughts.

What we're getting at is that you shouldn't try to create anything when you are not in vibrational alignment. Keep in mind, the Vibrational Vortex of Creation doesn't respond to your *words.* It responds to your matching vibration or your emotional state of being. It responds to the *feelings* that are generated from your thoughts.

If you are not in the Vortex, you only have one thing to do. Get in there! So how do you get in there if you're not? Simple. Let go of whatever thoughts and actions you are doing that are keeping you out of it! Those things that you are doing and thinking all day every day that are affecting your vibration most of the time.

We're not talking about the things that are going on "out there" in the world. Remember, we live in an inside-out world, not an outside-in world. We're talking about the things that are going on "in here," in your mind. They are the things you're thinking about and ruminating about most of the time, the negative beliefs and definitions you're holding on to.

Here's is what I am trying to impart to you. When you learn to live with *less on your mind*, your negative, scary, or unsettling thoughts will just flow through you and you'll stop resisting life. You won't get caught up in your old, contaminated thinking. And when you stop resisting life, you automatically align with your Authentic Self and drop back into the Vibrational Vortex of Creation.

When you enjoy your life, when you enjoy what makes you feel good, when you interact with those whom you love, when you make long lists of things you appreciate, you automatically drop back into the Vibrational Vortex of Creation.

Here's the big idea I want you to capture that will make the most difference to you. It's when you say to yourself, "Somehow, someway I'm going to continue to have less and less on my mind and bring myself into the vibrational vicinity of who I really am—being myself, enjoying life, and feeling good. And when I am in that place of non-resistance and I'm feeling good, then I will set my goals. Then I will make my plans. Then I will call the airlines and book my flight. Then I will ask for a raise. Then I will ask that person out on a date. Then I will go to the store and purchase new clothes. Then I will make love to the person I love. Then I will make that phone call."

In other words, get into the Vibrational Vortex *first*, get into a good feeling *first*, and *then* go after what you want.

Contradictory Energy vs. Desire

Contradictory Energy is the biggest obstacle to creating the things you desire in your life. Contradictory Energy is when your desire causes you to go one way and your doubt causes you to go another way. And because you've got this *equal energy pulling against itself*, you don't go anywhere.

If you're like most people, the more you want something, the more you keep noticing you don't have it or it hasn't shown up in your life yet. You have your energy going in opposing directions—*wanting* and *not having*—and you feel stressed because you're pulling against yourself. But understand this: only you can pull against yourself. There are no other forces preventing you, hindering you, or working against you. There are just your thoughts and what they are doing to you.

What most people don't realize is that it takes a lot of focusing on *what you don't want* to keep you from going in the direction of *what you do want*. But that's easy to understand because we've been trained to be objective, to weigh up the pros and the cons, the pluses and the minuses, and to be "realistic." And anytime you do that, you're trying to create from your intellect and your conditioned personal mind. However, in order to create the best possible outcome in any situation, what you want are new ideas, new solutions, new possibilities, and new opportunities. And trust me, you won't find them in your old thinking.

Your non-physical, expanded Authentic Self is aware of where you're standing right now in relation to what you desire. And because it lives in a reality of possibility and expansiveness, the only reason you can ever feel positive or negative emotion is because you're either in alignment with it or you're pushing against it.

This is a very important point: to understand and accept that negative feelings and emotions are not a bad thing. Why? Because your negative feelings and emotions are a **feedback mechanism** designed to let you know that your expanded Authentic Self feels differently about whatever it is you're focusing on when those negative feelings and emotions are present. Any negative feelings or emotions you experience in life are telling you that your Authentic Self is thinking something different. In other words, your Authentic Self is coming up against your contaminated thinking or your Ego Self.

Let's say you've been focusing on something that has caused you negative emotion and you've been participating in it long enough that your negative emotion is really strong. You have a very strong negative opinion, attitude, or perspective about it. And whenever you focus on it, you feel a strong negative emotion. That means whatever you are focusing on, your Authentic Self has a *different perspective* about it because it's seeing it through the eyes of the deeper Intelligence behind life, not your contaminated thinking.

For example, you might say, "I just hate that person" or "I hate this situation." If you understand how this feedback mechanism works, your dislike or hatred for someone or something is an indication that your Authentic Self feels *very different* about it and *it is not going join you in that negative perspective*. So, when you have any negative feelings or emotions, stop and just think for a moment, "I wonder what my Authentic Self, who I really am at my core, is thinking about this because clearly it's different than what I'm thinking, otherwise I wouldn't be feeling this way."

As you continue to have less and less on your mind and you're not analysing, not trying to bang everything into palace, your Authentic Self will tend to it. In fact, if you get out of the way, it's a done deal! However, most people don't think it's "done" until there is a physical manifestation that everybody can see. So, as they look at the physical world as it currently exists, they lose their point of attraction and end up going in the wrong direction. They are not in the receiving mode of new ideas, new solutions, and new possibilities that will bring their desire into physical reality.

What happens so often is that we have an inner sense or intuition that what we desire is coming together and we get on the receiving mode for a little while. Then when we don't see everything coming together, we start taking unnecessary actions to try to force the outcome—and then we lose our connection. Essentially, we're back where we started. What we're missing is that the deeper Intelligence of our Authentic Self is informing us that it's in the process of bringing us all the *cooperative components* we need, but we have to be in the receptive mode to receive them. What this means is that we just have to get out of our own way and allow the physical and non-physical aspects to work together to effortlessly bring whatever we desire into physical manifestation.

Understanding How the Physical and Non-Physical Aspects of Your Life are Working Together

Your Authentic Higher Self—the energy from which you came from and will return to—is always present and active within you. This is the larger, more *expansive* part of you. And just as the physical aspect of you attracts what you focus on, the non-physical aspect of you—your expanded Authentic Self—attracts what it focuses on too. So, in every moment that you are conscious, awake, and focused in your physical body, you are a point of attraction, but at the same time, the non-physical aspect of you is also a point of attraction. There are always **two points of attraction** going on at the same time, so it's to your advantage to blend them together.

The non-physical aspect of you—your Authentic Higher Self—is always focused on your further evolution. When you focus on "more"—more love, more appreciation, more money, more clarity, more of anything—that "more" of whatever you have asked for is being processed.

The non-physical aspect of you goes into action because the physical aspect of you has asked for more. This is what the evolution of all species is about. So, the non-physical aspect of you is operating in this more expansive place that we are calling the Vibrational Vortex of Creation and the vibrational attraction of whatever you are asking for is responding to you in that more expansive place or environment.

The difference between your expanded Authentic Self and your Physical Self (which includes your ego and your personal mind) is that your expanded Authentic Self does not contradict its own desires. It is not conflicted. But when the physical aspect of you lives in contradiction, it causes separation—not between you and what you want, but between you and the expanded version of you.

When the physical aspect of you is thinking a thought that harmonizes with the knowing of your expanded Authentic Self, the emotion you feel is one of *clarity, love, joy, passion, excitement, and satisfaction.* But when you are thinking a thought that is opposing or contradicting what your expanded Authentic Self knows to be true, then you feel agitation, uneasiness, overwhelm, blame, guilt, anger, fear, worry, or some other negative emotion, even physical illness.

Every emotion you feel is happening in the now, the now of you that is functioning in the physical and the now of you functioning in the non-physical, *at the same time.* The difference is that your expanded Authentic Self, the non-physical aspect of you, is not thinking about your past or your future. It's focused on you *right here and right now.* It's always moving forward with you when life causes you to want something more. And then when you launch your desire, your expanded Authentic Self is all over it! Knowing it, holding the light, and holding its attention upon it.

The Universe or the Formless Intelligence behind life is responding to that by gathering all the cooperative components to this new creation. The question is: are you going along with it? And your answer can be always be found in your *feelings* and *your emotions.*

If you have less on your mind and you feel calm and settled, the answer is "Yes." You are going along with your new expansion. But if you feel negative emotion and your mind is filled with contaminated thinking, then you are not going along with it—at least not right now. Right now, you are not only caught up in your thinking and limited beliefs, but you are not letting them go. This signal or feedback mechanism is telling you that you're out of alignment with your desire and that you are getting in your own way!

When this happens, see it as an opportunity to let any contradictory thoughts go. There's nothing else you need to do. As soon as you let them go, you will have less on your mind again. When you have a clear, uncluttered mind, you will automatically be back in alignment with your desire. You can expect your desire to not only show up and manifest in the best possible way, but with the least amount of resistance.

The Power Behind Deliberate Creation

We have been conditioned to think that we have to work hard and struggle to get what we want. This is because the formula that most people try to create their lives from is: **do + have = be**.

The idea behind this is if I *do* enough stuff and take enough action then I will *have* what I want. When I finally *have* what I want then I will *be* rich, *be* happy, *be* confident, *be* successful, or whatever the state of "Being" is.

We buy into the mindset that "doing" is the key element and if we are not doing something, we are never going to get anywhere. However, the formula behind Deliberate Creation works on an entirely different model which is: **be + do = have**.

Notice what comes first: to "be." This refers to your state of *Being*: being yourself and being in the flow of life.

For a long time, my state of being was focusing on what I didn't have. I was chasing after everything I didn't have. This caused me to live in a state of being that was low vibration. Then when I was *doing*, the actions I took would frustrate me and I would struggle.

In the end, I was having more of the same thing. In other words, my awareness was on what I didn't have and trying to improve myself and my situation from that state of *Being*. My state of being was coming from "not enough." Therefore, no matter what I did or what actions I took, I was having more of the same thing: not enough!

When I learned how this worked and started being non-resistant, being myself, being comfortable with who I am, being what I prefer to be and living in a state of being with *less on my mind*, everything changed. If you really understand this, life can be so much simpler.

The thing I want you to focus on the most is the *Being* aspect. The "do" or the "doing" will become obvious and the "have" will take care of itself. The problem is that we get caught up in the doing. There's this whole idea that I need to *do* this in order to *have* that so my focus is on what strategies or techniques I will use or what actions I will take to make that happen.

Doing is effective and necessary at a particular level of frequency. However, there's another level of frequency that supersedes doing. There's another octave up that scale which is the *Being* state. The *Being* state is a higher vibration than the doing state.

Now, we don't get to bypass the *doing*; however, we're not using the action of doing to force the outcome or to try to get into the *Being* state. Doing doesn't always have to be physical action. It can be the thought you are thinking or the feeling you are feeling. That is still action. If you need to take physical action, it will be inspired and obvious and won't be coming from a place of fear or lack.

When you are in the *Being* state, it creates a natural desire. Once your Physical Self and your non-physical expanded Authentic Self are aligned with your natural desire, it will inform you of what you need to do and how to do it, and that gives birth to inspired action. The actions you take will depend on your state of being.

The first step is to always focus on your state of *Being*. This puts you in a state of "doing without doing" or "action without effort." And in that state, you magnetize synchronicities, attract opportunities, and leverage your inner resources.

Now, in order for this to work, you have to learn to ignore what other's call "reality." When people say to you, "You need to face reality," your response should be, "I don't *face* reality, I *create* reality." One is *passive* and the other is *active*.

I know we're conditioned to respond to "reality" or the circumstances outside of us, but you must do the opposite. Ignore "reality" and focus on your *internal vibration* and your *emotional state*. Check to make sure you are not getting caught up in your thinking. Make sure your personal, ego-driven mind is not trying to run the show, telling you to be "realistic" or trying to get you to focus on your circumstances and how difficult it's going to be to create what you desire.

Keep reminding yourself of this important truth: *My circumstances do not determine my state of Being. My state of Being determines my circumstances.*

Another way of saying this is:

"Circumstances don't matter. What matters is my state of Being."

Say it to yourself now and listen to the way that synchronistically translates.

"Circumstances don't matter. What matters is my state of Being."

It's a play on words. Circumstances don't *matter*. In other words, what's going on outside of me does not create *matter* or materialization. What matters is my state of *Being*. Only my state of *Being* can materialize my experience.

So anytime you find yourself doubting or fearful because of what you believe the situation is or what your circumstances are, remind yourself: *"Circumstances don't matter. What matters is my state of Being."* And then choose the state of *Being* you prefer.

If you try to force the outcome in any situation, you will continue to struggle. But when you are in your preferred state of *Being*, new inspiration, new ideas, new opportunities, and new people will show up in your life. That's the "Dance of Synchronicity."

Before I understood how we are designed to live, which is in a state of *Being* with *less on our mind* until we receive the intuition or wisdom on what to do next, I would be doing, doing, doing all the time. In other words, I wasn't a human *"Being,"* I was a human *"doing!"*

And then it occurred to me that everything that I have accomplished in my life that I'm truly proud of came to me without effort. Now, there was *work* involved, but no effort. And if you look at your life, you will see this pattern as well. If you look at the things you've accomplished that you're truly proud of, whether it's a skill you acquired, an education, a personal accomplishment, or an artistic accomplishment, if it's something that really gives *meaning* to your life and *fulfils you*, notice it came to you without a lot of effort. In other words, you didn't have to force the outcome.

Now that doesn't mean you didn't have to *work* at it, but there is a huge difference between *working* at something and *efforting* at it. When you are efforting at something, you are living in a state of fear and you are trying to force the outcome. When you work at it, you just do what you need to do next without any fear and without any effort.

When I look back, anything I efforted at or tried to force was not only frustrating, but I didn't feel good even if I accomplished it. And that's how it works. When we have less on our mind and our mind is clear and uncluttered, new opportunities, new solutions, new ideas, and new synchronicities will show up. So, the simple message here is that in order to live a magical life without a lot of effort, we need to focus on our state of *Being* and let that guide us to the next step.

The Spider Principle of "Do Nothing to Attract Everything"

Most people I know don't like spiders, but spiders have a very important lesson to teach us about *Being* and not doing. Spiders live by the concept of "Do Nothing to Attract Everything." Spiders don't *do* anything. They just set up their web, wait for a fly to hit the web, and just follow the vibration to where the fly landed. This is actually the way we are designed to live. It's just a matter of where and how we set up our web.

So how do you set up your web? First, you must be clear on your intention. Exactly who or what would you like to attract into your web?

Many people set up their web online using social media. They want to attract people who are interested in what they have to offer or share. That's one way to do it, but I've found one of the most powerful ways to set up your web is to go out and meet new people. Set up your web in places where you might meet that special person, or overhear a conversation, or even meet someone who will introduce you someone else who can take you in a different direction.

Whether you're using the Spider Principle to create a personal web or business web, you are creating an opportunity for synchronicity to come into your life. All you are doing is just being like a spider. You are clear on your intention and you are just *Being* yourself. When the flies land in your web, all you have to do is just follow the vibration. More often than not, you will be surprised at what has landed in your web that you may have never considered or thought possible.

Trust me, if you are sitting at home planning your future, waiting for something to happen, you are not catching any flies. If you set up your web in a place where there are no flies, you are going to starve. For me, I want to have powerful conversations with people. Your web might be going out and talking with people—not just online, but in real life—who are genuinely interested in what you are interested in or are interested in you!

You have to set up your web in the right places where people can see you and connect with you and offer you opportunities that can just flow into your web naturally. Anything you are doing to just *Be* yourself, share yourself, and follow your passion and your highest joy will attract people, situations, and opportunities into your web.

This is the Spider Principle of "Do Nothing to Attract Everything." It works for spiders, it works for me, and it will work for you! I invite you to play with this idea a little and you'll be surprised and delighted at what will be attracted to your web!

The "Obstacle Illusion"

By now you may be saying, "Okay I agree with you so far, but you don't understand. This is all well and fine, but I'm stuck. I cannot see any possible solution."

What's happening is that you are temporarily stuck in what I call an "Obstacle Illusion." The Obstacle Illusion is setting up an obstacle or an illusion in your mind that believes there is only one solution to your situation. For example, let's say that you think all your problems could be solved with more money. However, if you focus *just on money* as your solution, you're limiting your definition of what other possibilities are available to you. Money is only one possibility. You need to expand your understanding to see that there are more resources available to you than you are able to see at the moment because you are caught up in your obstacle illusion.

The first step to attracting more money or any other resource you need is connecting with your highest *joy,* your *passion,* your *excitement,* and your *creativity*. This is always the first step. Then *stay* in the vibrational energy of what you *prefer* instead of living in a fearful vibration of what you don't prefer.

Once again, I need to remind you that we live in a vibrational universe and your **emotional vibration** is everything! When you stay in the vibrational energy of what you prefer, you are open to receive *new* ideas, *new* solutions, *new* thoughts, and *new* opportunities on how you can live your dream without necessarily having the resources you might have thought were necessary.

And before I continue, therein lies a very important point. You cannot live in the *opposite* state of being or vibrational frequency of what you prefer and hope everything will just show up in spite of it. If you don't stay in your preferred state of *Being,* you will not be capable of receiving *new* ideas, *new* solutions, *new* thoughts, and *new* opportunities that will show you how you can move forward, because they'll be invisible to you. Those doors will be closed to you.

You see, every state of *Being* is a choice. If you make the choice to live in the state of fear, you are going to shut yourself off from receiving the wisdom and inspiration you need from the deeper Intelligence of your expanded Authentic Self. So, if you are afraid because you have no other resources or you are afraid because you've lost your resources, you are shutting yourself off from the Intelligence that will guide you and show you what you need to do next.

So, you constantly need to remind yourself that living in the state of *Being* or the vibrational frequency of your highest *joy*, your *passion*, your *excitement*, and what you feel *inspired to create* is the most effortless way to turn things around and have your desire show up in your life.

Now, as you're reading this, there is probably a part of your brain (the rational or critical faculty) that will bring up all the reasons why this is nonsense and why it won't work for you. It may work for *others*, but not for *you*—because your situation is "different."

Now let me stop you here. I want you to understand something very important. I don't even know you, but, in some sense, I can read your thoughts. You think everything I've just said is a "nice idea" and it would be great if it actually worked, but it won't work for you. Well, to be quite frank, that thought is incredibly arrogant.

It's incredibly arrogant to say that the principle of Deliberate Creation that works for everyone else on the planet can't work for you. Essentially, you are singling yourself out. What you are saying is that out of All Creation, you are the *exception*.

I know you don't intentionally want to be arrogant. You think you are being "realistic," but here's the problem: while you may think you are being "realistic," the idea that "it may be true for others but won't work for me" is going to keep you stuck where you are.

All you need to do is understand that this is the way Creation is structured for everybody. No exceptions! Not even you! This is the way our reality is created whether you believe it or not. In fact, it's working for you all the time because what you are putting out is what you are going to get back.

The *certainty* you are putting out that it's not realistic for you—or even worse, that you don't deserve it—is what you are getting back. But here's the good news in all of that: if you don't have what you want, you are living proof that it does work! You are putting out doubt, fear, and uncertainty and you are getting back doubtful, fearful, and uncertain outcomes. So, it does work! It is self-proven!

If you are struggling and don't know what to do or feel you don't have the resources to do something, it's because when we put out doubtful, fearful, and uncertain vibrations, it mirrors back our thoughts and beliefs and makes them seem real. It's a trick of the mind. Don't fall for it! Wake up from the toxic trance of doubt, fear, and uncertainty and realize *you are making it all up*. And more good news is that because you're making everything up, *you can make up something else!* In other words, at any moment in time, you are always *just one thought away* from changing the direction of your life.

Now when I share this with people, they will often say, "Okay, that sounds reasonable, I'll try it."

Trying is the excuse we use when we're unsure that we are going to be able to achieve our outcome. Trying presupposes the possibility of failure. Trying works like an insurance policy. You're insuring your Ego Self against failure. So, if you do something and it doesn't work out for you, you can cash in your insurance policy against failure. The one that says, "I tried, but it's not my fault that it didn't work out." And of course, no one can blame you. After all, you tried! This lets you off the hook with yourself and others. The only problem is that trying is crap!

Here's the true definition of **trying**: trying is the amount of time you believe you need before you *actually commit* to doing something.

And I'll tell you a secret. I know *exactly* the moment when you will do it. The moment you will do it is the moment you are tired of *not* doing it. When you decide things will change, things will change. When you're are sick and tired of being sick and tired, you will change. Until you decide things will change, things will say the same. Put simply, if something is important to you, you will find a **way**. If not, you will find an **excuse**.

If you keep "trying", you will always be frustrated, tired, and disappointed. The bottom line is that you either trust the deeper wisdom of your expanded Authentic Self and take the next step, or you don't. And once you do, things will start to change. I promise you that.

What if it Still Looks Like Your Circumstances are Not Changing?

When you raise your inner vibrational energy and your state of Being, things *can* and *often will* start to change very rapidly. As a result, your physical reality will mirror that change. However, you may still see the same scenarios around you, or it will look like nothing is changing. If that happens, don't assume you're doing something "wrong" or it's "not working."

This is where our personal mind and our ego can sometimes get caught up in their own sense of control. Your personal mind looks at physical reality as being the only "real" thing there is and it will assume that if it does not see an exact, one-to-one reflection or change in the circumstances that surround you, there must be something wrong, or you failed, or it's not working.

However, it always works, but here's what's happening. When people think that something is wrong or it's not working, they haven't taken into consideration that sometimes there is a time lag for creation or manifestation to show up in physical reality. Certain things need to line up first that they are not aware of. However, they view this time lag as an obstacle. And as soon as they do that, they are right back where they started.

What they are missing is that it's not just about focusing on what you desire and staying in that positive vibrational energy and *waiting* for something to happen. If you're waiting for something to happen, you will experience the time lag as an obstacle. You will get frustrated and think to yourself, "It's not working." But it is working! Everything is working or unfolding as it should. If you try to control the outcome, you will only delay it—or worse yet, create something you don't want. All you need to do is relax, let it unfold, and enjoy the journey as much as you can!

And a little tip here. It is not about "I'm enjoying my life right now, but it can't compare to what I'm waiting for." If you're *waiting*, you're not *living*. Life is about the ongoing experience itself. As many people have said: "The process is the point. The journey is the destination." Life is not about trying to get somewhere else. It's about being *here* more often and having an awareness of the present moment.

Living your magic is an art form. And the first part of that art form to master is simply being here now with whatever's happening in your life and trusting that what's happening is happening for a reason—otherwise it wouldn't be happening! So, if you are willing to accept that whatever is happening is happening for the purpose of putting you in touch with more of yourself so that you can expand your reflection of yourself, you can be excited about anything the process has to show you. This means nothing is "wrong," nothing is "negative," and nothing is "not working."

Instead of struggling with what's happening in the moment or waiting for something better to happen in the future, you can experience whatever is happening in the moment as part of you creating your art. You're the artist! By *being* the artist, by *being* the art piece itself, you are willing to accept that everything that is happening is necessary for you to create your art. If you understand this, you can step back and learn what it is trying to teach you so that you can expand your reflection of yourself and create *an even more magnificent art piece.*

Whatever is happening in your life, whatever you perceive as positive or negative is *always* something that will increase your understanding of who and what you are as a co-creator and a reality-shaper. If you look at it that way and stay in that energy, believe me, very quickly you will expand in many different directions and your reality will expand as well.

Understand you have a choice about the way you're experiencing your life right now. You can experience it either as an obstacle or as part of the unfolding of your highest *joy*, your *passion*, and your *creativity*. Whatever is happening, even if it seems like an obstacle, is a stepping stone. It is a piece of it. It's not apart from it. And if you understand that it's part of the process, you will experience this timeframe as part of the unfolding of your desire coming together instead of waiting for something better to happen.

And when you stop waiting for something better to happen, guess what? It *happens* because you are no longer *waiting* for it to happen. You take the waiting out of the equation by enjoying the journey and the unfolding of your desire so much that you collapse and compress time. And before you know it, something else is happening and then something else is happening, and you are there! Often in a much better place or outcome than you could have possibly imagined!

There's no waiting when you start doing what you prefer and living in your highest *joy*, your *passion*, your *love*, and your *creativity*. Those things do not contain the component of waiting. If you begin to see that all your experiences along the way are equal, then you won't be waiting for any one particular experience, because you are always in the right place at the right time, so it doesn't matter what's happening. You bypass the Obstacle Illusion and you seamlessly create the reality you desire while enjoying your mind and enjoying the journey.

Cleaning Up Your Vibration

We have been talking a lot about vibrational alignment. The definition of vibrational alignment is having *desire* and *no resistance*. The goal is to let go of any resistant thoughts or beliefs that are getting in your way. You do that *by having less and less on your mind and allowing the thoughts that you don't like to just pass through you.* And as you do that, you will automatically spend more time focusing on what you prefer. The more time you give to what you prefer, naturally the less time you will be giving to what you don't prefer. That's the way you clean up your vibration.

Remember, whenever you have a negative perspective or negative emotion, the purpose it serves is to remind you that you are choosing something that is not in alignment with the way your Inner Being or your Authentic Self is seeing it. It will never join you in that because it has a broader perspective. Your Authentic Self—who you truly are—will never get caught up in your toxic trances. So anytime you have a negative perspective or negative emotion, it serves as a feedback mechanism to let you know you are out of alignment with who you are and who you choose to be.

Another reason we are not being who we are or not being who we choose to be is that we often contour our thoughts and behaviours to match what other people want from us, but the problem is that different people want different things from us, so we get confused. And the thing that's most difficult about that (and is detrimental to you) is when you look to others for their approval or you empathize with what they believe so that you can be in harmony with them, you are getting further and further away from who you really are.

And it doesn't matter how good a case somebody else makes or how convincing they are. Anybody who has you focused on what you *don't want* is calling you away from who you are. And in the end, you are going to suffer.

Keep in mind that every person out there is a hypnotist. They just don't call themselves that. There are well-meaning, well-intentioned friends, family, and even "experts" who are trying to hypnotize you into believing they know what is best for you. But no one can know what is best for you but you. So, you have to focus on what you want, not what other people want or what they think is best for you.

When I share this, sometimes people will say to me, "What you teach is selfishness. It's all about you."

And I tell them, "That's absolutely right!" Because if you are not selfish enough to stay in alignment with who you are, then you don't have anything of value to give to anyone else. Staying in alignment with who you are, your

Authentic Self, allows you to live in a non-resistant flow of life. And deep down, this is what everyone truly wants!

Doing What Comes Naturally

I often ask people, "What do you want?"

You would be surprised at how many respond by saying, "I don't really know what I want."

Then I rephrase the question. "Okay, tell me what don't want."

And as soon as I ask that question, they're off and running: "I don't want to be broke," "I don't want to be alone," "I don't want to be without a job or a career," or "I don't want (fill in the blank)."

The first thing this tells me is that they don't understand the purpose of **contrast**. Once again, contrast is there to show us what we don't want so we'll be inspired to move towards what we do want.

I believe that at a deeper level everyone knows what they want. Everyone has a passion and a **natural desire**. Sometimes it may be hidden, but it can easily be uncovered. And that's your starting point.

Here are five Questions to help you discover your passion and your natural desire.

1. What do you love to learn about? It doesn't necessarily have to be in a formal education or training. It could be anything. What do you love to learn about yourself?
2. What do you like to excel in? What would you like to become better at?
3. What do you like to talk about? What topic is always coming up for you? When you are with your friends or with a group of people, where do you like to lead the conversation? What do you want other people to know about?

4. What would you love to get paid for? If I told you right now that I would give you five thousand dollars a week for whatever it is you would love to get paid for, what would be your answer?
5. If you would like to be of service to others, how would you do it? What makes you feel good when you help others in this way?

If you answer these questions, you will notice there's a common thread running between them and you'll be able to connect the dots between the answers. There will be similarities in your answers.

The answer that feels "right" will be a high vibration activity that comes naturally to you. You will begin to see that's what you should be putting your focus on. And when you follow it, new opportunities and new possibilities will open up for you. Take the time to do this. I think you'll find it highly enjoyable!

THE MAGICAL POWER OF GRATITUDE

I f you truly want to live your magic, one of the things you must consider is the magical power of gratitude. Gratitude is one of the highest vibrations of thought. When you live in the state of gratitude, you are creating an opportunity for synchronicity to come into your life.

However, it's not easy to be grateful when you're struggling, especially when your thoughts keep creating the same experiences in your life that "prove" how difficult life can be. Now, if we want to "prove" to ourselves that life is a struggle, it's pretty easy to do. On the other hand, if we want to "prove" to ourselves that life is not a struggle, that's easy to do as well because our life mirrors our thoughts.

Here is why gratitude is so powerful. You cannot be *in* a state of gratitude and *out* of the "flow of life" at the same time. It is not possible. Gratitude is one of the most flow-producing emotions we can experience.

The amount of gratitude you have is directly proportional to your baseline level of happiness. The less gratitude you have, the unhappier you will be. In other words, if you increase the amount of gratitude you have in your life, you will automatically experience an increase in your baseline level of happiness. But it gets even better!

When you increase your baseline level of happiness, you also increase the opportunity for synchronicity to come into your life. You literally become irresistible to your desires. The floodgates of synchronicity open up and the people, circumstances, and things you desire start to flow to you easily and effortlessly.

This is not just New Age nonsense. It's a scientific fact. It's been measured in university laboratories by hooking up EKG machines to participants. The results showed that when the participants were in a state of sincere gratitude and appreciation, they were psychologically and physiologically in a state of electromagnetic alignment.

Unfortunately, gratitude or appreciation is not a state that most of us experience habitually. It is something we have to learn and practice like any other habit. By developing a **daily practice**—for just ten minutes per day— you can retrain your brain to look for everything possible to be grateful for. And what you will find is that for every minute invested in gratitude and appreciation, you will be paid back one hundred-fold in terms of peace of mind, abundance, and increased well-being.

It's as simple as making a gratitude list on a small notepad before you start your day. You can do this while having breakfast instead of watching the news, reading the paper, or staring at your smartphone. This sets the tone for the day. You will be amazed at how it will change your baseline level of happiness. And instead of being an Unconscious Reactor to the external events around you, you become a Conscious Creator.

When you make your list, you can include your material possessions, the money you have right now, your health, your career, your relationships, where you live, even the little things in life like a comfortable bed to sleep in or the fact that you have enough food to eat. Even if some of these things are not the way you want them to be right now, you are expressing gratitude for what you already have.

If you have a problem coming up with enough items on your list, it means that you have things in your life that you are still resisting. Perhaps it's your boss with the bad attitude, your car that won't start, your volatile teenage stepdaughter, your ex, the government, the blemish on your face that won't go away, or the bills that keep piling up.

You may also feel a lot of resistance to some of the people or conditions on that list, but here's the important point: it's your *resistance* that is making it difficult for you to get what you want or heal these circumstances. Resistance to anything will keep it away from you and push it out of your life. Take a moment to look at the things and people in your life that bother you or upset you and decide that you are going to stop resisting them.

The power of gratitude works in every area of your life, both in the material world and in the psychological world. Be grateful for the new insights you're gaining. Gratitude promotes new insights. When you live in a feeling of gratitude for what you have already seen and understand, it attracts even more insights and understanding.

And next, in order to demonstrate that you are already living in the flow, every single day find some way to give somebody something that you already have. It can be big or small. Be a confident and enthusiastic giver and watch what happens!

One of the most powerful actions you can take is to give the very thing that you want to others. If there's something you feel you don't have enough of, then give that away. If you want more money, give money. If you want more time, give your time. If you want more love, give your love.

Truly successful and happy people give money, time, love, support, and encouragement because they are truly grateful for what they already have. They know that by giving, they open themselves up to receiving what they desire. What you are really doing is you are looking at everything you have in your life, not just as *stuff*, but as evidence of a flowing current, a river of abundance that has come into your life.

Let's go back to our definition of abundance: *the ability to attract what you need when you need it.* When you give to others, you are demonstrating your confidence that abundance will continue to flow into your life and you're grateful for it. Put simply, giving makes room for more abundance to come into your life. By giving gratefully, continuously, and consistently, life ceases to be a struggle because you are placing yourself in the flow of life and you become both an inlet and an outlet for the abundance to flow through.

Since we want to be grateful for everything, we must also include ourselves in the process. This means accepting our humanness and forgiving ourselves for all the mistakes and imperfections in our life. We need to be able to love that reflection in the mirror.

When you look in the mirror and pass judgment on what you see, you have no choice but to pass judgment on others as well. If you don't like the main character in your story, then everything and everyone in your story is subject to judgment. But if you accept your humanness and forgive yourself in spite of your mistakes and imperfections, you can accept and forgive others as well.

One of the experiences I like to create with with my clients is something I call "The Magic Mirror." This is an experience that is designed to get them to look at themselves in a positive light no matter what they've done or have not done, to look at themselves with unconditional love and non-judgment. Another way of saying this is to look at their True Nature.

Living Your Magic Beyond Social Conditioning

Unfortunately, there are certain individuals and groups in our society who often try to hijack our magic to keep us from living the life we desire. They want to lead us in another direction. The news media and the entertainment industry in particular try to hijack our magic by brainwashing us to think we need to focus on something other than being ourselves and creating what we prefer.

The news media feeds us this idea that the world is a scary place. They focus on negativity and try to scare us so that we feel agitated and anxious most of the time. Have you ever asked yourself why the news is almost always negative? The psychological principle behind negative news is that when people are agitated, worried, or stressed out, they consume more. When they are relatively happy and content, they consume less.

If you watch the news, expect to be told about the negative, scary situations that are happening locally or internationally *that you have no control over* so they can build up your anxiety level. Then, expect to have the solution to your anxiety sold back to you. The solution is always some form of *relief* which coincidently happens to be the products and services that are advertised during the commercial break that will temporarily make you feel better until the next newscast.

Personally, I don't watch the news because it breeds a certain level of insanity. If you look around you, you can see how people can get caught up in it. For example, terrorism. The problem is that there is very little we can do about it or stop it. However, the fact is that in most western countries, more people are killed by automobiles every year than are killed by terrorists. I am not making light of the people who have died from terrorism, but we need to put the problem into perspective.

Another reason I don't watch the news is because I don't want to spread the fear by talking about it with others. Instead, I choose to teach people that our fearful experience of life does not come from the outside-in. It comes from the inside-out. This allows them to inoculate themselves against fear. And regardless of what happens, if you don't buy into the assumption "that's the way the world is," at the very least, you are much better equipped to deal with whatever happens. This includes terrorism.

I have found there is another benefit to ignoring all this fear and negativity. And that is, in my own life, somehow when I settle down, the people around me seem to settle down too. Somehow, when something stops looking terrifying to me, the people around me are less terrified. I'm not exactly sure how that works, and I guess I don't need to know, but I see it all the time.

If I still want to waste my time and energy watching the news and scaring myself, I can, but I also know that how I feel in the moment I'm watching it is based on my thinking and perception about it, not what I'm watching on the screen. If I know what's going on inside of me, I am not going to be fooled by it. And I am certainly going to do a lot better than if I think it is coming at me instead of from me.

Another way society tries to hijack our magic is by creating a narcissistic culture that compels us to look at other people and compare ourselves to them. We're living in a narcissistic culture that is obsessed with celebrities. Celebrity is everything these days, especially for teenagers and Millennials.

When you ask people in this age bracket, "What is your dream" or "What would you like to do with your life?" the answer you hear most often is to be rich and famous. This idea is reinforced on TV reality shows where people are competing to be rich and famous in six to eight weeks. Being "famous" and getting a lot of attention from others is the epitome of our culture. This is the power of celebrity.

Through the power of celebrity, the entertainment industry trains our brain to focus on and worship people (often stupid people) who are rich and famous. The entertainment industry literally *creates* these celebrities and puts them in front of us so that we don't focus on who we truly are, but instead are encouraged to be like them, dress like them, and follow them on social media. This means we will spend more money purchasing whatever these celebrities are wearing, selling, or promoting.

On top of this, we watch reality TV shows where people make fools of themselves so that we can feel better about ourselves. All of this is the dumbing down of who we really are and keeps us from living our magic.

If you want to live your magic, you have to turn your attention *away* from these people and follow your own path. Without focusing on what these celebrities are doing—or for that matter even caring about it—trust me, you'll find yourself living beyond the conditioning and brainwashing of popular culture and you will have a magical life!

Living with Less on Your Mind

Throughout this book, I have repeatedly talked about living with less on your mind. The reason for that is that when you have less on your mind, it allows more magic and synchronicity to show up in your life.

However, having less on our mind or having nothing on our mind doesn't mean our mind is blank. It means we have a Presence of Mind. We're living in the present moment and in alignment with our inner creative wisdom.

When I talk about having less on our mind or having nothing on our mind, I am often asked, "So how do I do that?"

People try all kinds of different techniques to accomplish this. One of the most popular is "Mindfulness." You can find entire books and courses on it. Mindfulness is usually practiced as nonjudgmental focus of attention on one's emotions, thoughts, and sensations that are occurring in the present moment. However, there is also another way to look at mindfulness that can be understood on a different level. The way I look at mindfulness is that mindfulness is not something we have to *practice* because it's a *naturally-occurring mental state* that happens when our heads aren't filled up with a lot of personal thinking.

Many people also practice meditation to quiet their mind. Many years ago, I learned Transcendental Meditation from the Maharishi Mahesh Yogi. I was one of his original students. When I meditated, sometimes I would get the benefit of being quieter and less stressed for a while but then I found that I would have to keep coming back and do it again and again to get to that same place. Finally, I came to the understanding that there is a fundamental difference between the "state" of meditation and being in a "meditative state."

Suddenly I realized that I didn't need to practice meditation to get there. Rather, it was the amount of time I could spend on a daily basis with less on my mind in the present moment. In other words, we can access that "state" on a regular basis whether we are meditating or not because, as it turns out, the meditative state is also a *naturally-occurring mental state* when we have less on our mind. It is not something we have to practice or do in order to get temporary relief.

The problem with any formal practice of mindfulness or mediation is it becomes another *doing* process. We are doing it to get to a quiet place. What I understand now is there is nothing to do! Like enlightenment, you don't have to try to *become* enlightened. It's simply a matter of recognizing you are *already* enlightened when you get out of your own way and have less on your mind.

If you want to practice mindfulness, meditation, or spend time in nature and go for a walk that's fine, but the more you try to use anything to get to a quiet place, the further away it will get from you. It's not that taking a walk, mindfulness, meditation, or doing any other practice isn't helpful. They certainly can be, but if you are using them to get to some place where you can quiet your mind and feel better, then it becomes another doing process. We are not designed to do anything to get to a place that's totally natural. There is nothing to do but to let go of our thinking. Letting go of our thinking is natural. It happens to every one of us every single day.

Perhaps you are asking, "How do I let go of my thinking?"

Well, let me ask you a question: "How do you fall asleep?" It's a natural process! In a sense, when you fall asleep, you have to give yourself permission to fall asleep. I've learned if we're caught up in our thinking, we can give ourselves *permission* to just *let go* and not fuse with our thoughts. It's as simple as that.

The key behind letting go of any thought is to see it for what it is. It's always something you are making up in the moment. For me it's, "Oh, I'm caught up in my thinking right now. I'm feeling anxious, worried, stressed, or whatever. I am going to let this go because it is not serving me in any way anyways!"

In other words, I am seeing my thought-generated perception as made-up and I'm giving myself permission to let go of my thinking in the moment.

When we have less on our mind, we fall into the Presence of Mind and we automatically stand with our True Authentic Self. Everything we do to try to quiet our mind and connect to the deeper wisdom of our True Authentic Self perpetuates the idea that we are disconnected. We can never be disconnected because there's no "on" or "off" switch. It's always "on" but we can't force it or try to get there because every time we say, "I am going to try to get there and quite my mind," we are caught up in our thinking again.

Once again, we need to remind ourselves that life is not about getting somewhere. We are already there! It's about recognizing we're already there and living moment-to-moment with less on our mind.

We are all human and at times we are going to get caught up in our thought storms. And when we do, we're going to feel insecure and a little bit unstable. It works like a snow globe. I'm sure you've seen a snow globe that has something inside of it like a snowman or a statue. The snow is a metaphor for your thinking. When you shake the globe or agitate your thinking, the globe is full of snow floating around and it's impossible to see the image inside the globe. If you stop shaking it, it settles down and you can see the image clearly though the glass, which is a metaphor for the mind. The logical conclusion? Stop shaking the snow globe of your mind and it will settle by itself!

When our mind settles down and we can accept our experience in the moment as something that will pass, we regain the ability to choose what thoughts we want to keep and which ones we want to let go. We learn to live in that space between stimulus and response.

It's interesting that we seem to intuitively know that our happy thoughts are nothing more than thoughts and we allow them to pass through us. But when it comes to our negative, scary, or limiting thoughts, we think that if we hold on to them long enough, they will somehow resolve our situation. Those are the thoughts we think have power by themselves, but they don't! We give them power. And when we do, we drop into a toxic trance.

When we are in a toxic trance, there are always warning signs. For me, it's when I start to take myself too seriously. It's when I think that what's happening in my life is now the center of the universe. When that happens, I know my thoughts have started to seem real to me and I've gone into a toxic trance. It's kind of a reminder that, "Dude, you're in a trance. Wake up!"

We all have a way of knowing when we've dropped into a toxic trance. When we can acknowledge, "I am caught up in my thinking and it seems real to me," it is much easier to get out of the trance. We are more inclined to let it pass because we know it's just a thought and the nature of thought is transient, which means there will be another one coming along in a minute, so I can let this one go!

The *less* we have on our mind, the *more* we're able to handle anything that comes our way with ease and grace. Another benefit is that we also tend to mess up our life less so there is less to process and clean up later when we become conscious again!

The Infinite Field of Possibility

One of the insights I like to share with people is that we live in an Infinite Field of Possibility. However, the limits of potential and possibility that we experience in our own lives and in the world are created in our own thinking.

We all have these invisible boundaries of thought that keep us stuck where we are. As they become visible, we can clearly see them for what they are, which is just stuff we are making up in our own imagination. The moment we see that we are the ones who have made up the edge of our own world is the moment our world expands. The moment we see that we are the ones who have decided not to look for new possibilities is the moment new things become possible.

Therefore, the only thing that stands between us and what we desire is our own misguided assumption or certainty that the world we see out there is "real" rather than a vividly-imagined projection of our mind.

This is not to suggest that there's no "real world" out there, but how we experience our world comes from the projection of our mind. The human experience only works in one way: from *thought* to *perception* to *experience*.

When we understand how the human system is constantly projecting our thoughts into our consciousness, enabling us to experience the effects of our thinking every single moment, we will no longer be fooled by the outside-in illusion.

However, at times we are still going to be fooled because whatever we are experiencing in the moment will *almost always* seem like it is directly connected to the outside world. When people come to me and tell me about their "problem" or their "situation," in their mind, the root cause is almost always some person, situation, or obstacle *outside* of them. And, it often looks like it is a seemingly intractable dilemma. Then I ask them, "Would you be willing for this situation to change?"

They always answer, "Yes." But right after the "Yes," they usually go on to explain why *it* can't change, or why *they* couldn't change.

Without even having to know the details or their personal history, I know they're stuck where they are because "situations" or "problems" do not exist in reality. We create what we call "situations" or "problems" in our life through our thought. We use thought to create a specific version of the world that we think is "real" out of the infinite possible versions waiting to be created.

It works like a video game. When you purchase a video game, all the different versions or possibilities of how the game will turn out are preprogrammed on the file. How we play the game determines the version or outcome we will end up with. Life works the same way. As we project a thought into consciousness, it brings our thinking to life. The projection is like a video game that allows us to experience the projections of our mind as if they're "real." This creates the illusion of a fixed, unchanging reality or a certain conclusion of "that's the way it is."

We see and feel what looks like the edge of the world or the edge of our limitation. Yet, think about this: what about the times when you've stepped over the edge of your perceived reality and survived or even thrived? Was it just luck, or could it be that the perceived "edges" of your world only exist in your own imagination?

Take a moment and think about where you're bumping up against the self-imposed limitations created by your own imagination. Look at the people and circumstances in your life where you think you already know what is possible and what is not. Could it be that you are making all that up?

Another way of saying this is: in what area or areas of your life are you trying to order from the *menu of limitation*, unaware that there is another menu, a full menu with something brand new, a *menu of possibility*, if only you would put in the order?

You see, it's what we think we know that holds us back. On the other hand, it's what we are open to being *wrong* about that opens up more possibilities and more options. When we open our minds to seeing something new, we inevitably see new things.

Ask yourself if you are open to seeing something new about the apparent edge of your world. This may be more difficult than you expect because most of us aren't really open to being wrong about the way we currently see "reality." Once you find the edges to your reality and you're willing to open up to seeing something new beyond it, prepare for your reality to change.

So how do we do this? I know I am stating the obvious, but in case you missed it: it's simply about trusting the inner creative wisdom of our Authentic Self that's doing its best to guide us moment-to-moment if we allow it.

Our connection to our Authentic Self is our connection with the deeper Intelligence behind life. Whatever we choose to call it, there *is* a deeper Intelligence behind our existence. There's no end or limitation to it, nor are there any boundaries. This Intelligence is constant and unchangeable and works through our Authentic Self. That's why it's reliable. On the other hand, our personal mind is always in a perpetual state of change. All humans have the inner ability to synchronize their personal mind with this deeper mind or Intelligence to access the wisdom they need whenever they need it.

We all connect with it in our own way. For me, I've learned to do less talking and more listening. By that I mean that instead of asking for solutions to my problems or wanting something to change in my life, I assume this deeper Intelligence already knows that!

Most of the time, the reason I am struggling is that I am missing something, or I am making something up that's keeping me out of alignment with reality. My job is to have less on my mind so the wisdom from the deeper Intelligence can come through my Authentic Self.

When I am willing to get out of my own way and give my personal thinking a rest, it almost always comes through as intuition and as a good feeling. I just *know* what to do next, or I *know* the answer.

If you're a religious person and you prefer to pray, you could do that too. However, real prayer is not about asking or pleading to an external God to help you get what you want or heal this, fix this, or change this so your life can be better. This deeper Intelligence already knows what you need or the lesson you need from this experience and what outcome is best for all concerned.

The *only* prayer you will ever need to pray is: "Show me the best way to handle this." Then shut up! You don't need to elaborate or fill in the details. It's about asking for a new way of looking at something so that you have a clearer understanding or a clearer direction of what to do next.

But I also need to tell you that sometimes the answer may come in a way you don't like or didn't expect. You may not like the answer or direction it is taking you because it is going to require you to look at and see things *differently*. The tendency is to resist it. Now you could say, "Well, that's great, but I don't like it. Is there another way?" But that's only going to take you right back to where you started. The idea is to be open to a new understanding and a new way of looking at things.

One thing is for sure. The one place you are not going to find new thinking is in a pile of old thinking. Old thinking is like having a bicycle with wheels that are out of alignment. You could get hurt if you try to ride it. If you don't take the time to straighten out the wheels and realign them, then you are just increasing your chance of getting hurt. If you are stuck and your life is not working, then your wheels need straightening out or you're going to continue to get hurt. You need new thoughts, new ideas, and new solutions but you're never going to find them in your old, contaminated thinking.

Who's Talking?

Another question you may be asking is, "How do I spot the difference between the wisdom of deeper Intelligence flowing through my Authentic Self and my own personal, ego-driven mind?"

In other words, is the wisdom of this deeper Intelligence actually coming through me or is it the voice of my ego-driven, personal mind?

The way I like to do it is to ask the question: "Who's talking?" If what I am hearing in my head is negative or it makes me feel bad, then I know it is the voice of my ego-driven, personal mind. If it is positive and makes me feel good, I know it is the wisdom of deeper Intelligence flowing through my Authentic Self.

True wisdom flowing through your Authentic Self is never about anything that's "wrong" with you. It doesn't try to convince you that you need to be "fixed" or you need to change anything *outside* of you. You just get a new insight about the situation. Then you get a new understanding. And once you have that, the change is easy, effortless, and natural because, once again, you are aligned with reality.

Wisdom is your direct connection to this deeper Intelligence behind life. And it is never going to come as an admonition. It is never going to come as a judgment. It is never going to come as something you need to "work on."

It is just the feeling of unconditional love without all the crap that there's something inherently wrong with you, or you're a bad person, or you're a sinner, or you need to be "fixed."

I don't care how messed up your life is right now or how bad you feel about yourself, there's absolutely nothing "wrong" with you! All that means is that you are human, and you have made some mistakes. Because of that, you are caught up in your contaminated thinking. It happens to all of us, but if you learn to recognize it as contaminated thinking and not place guilt, blame, shame, or judgment on yourself for your mistakes and you're willing to let go and start fresh, your life will immediately start to change for the better and you will start to live your magic once again.

Your Magnificent Self-Correcting System

When our life seems like it's "stuck" and we don't to know what to do next, that's our signal that we have gotten bogged down in our habitual and usually invisible thinking. When that happens, it's time to back off and stop reacting to the circumstances and people around us and allow our mind to self-correct and align with reality.

So how does this actually work? Most of us are familiar with our physical immune system. Our physical immune system is always endeavoring to self-correct and bring us back to a set point of innate physical health.

You may not be aware of it, but we also have a built-in psychological immune system that is always attempting to self-correct and to restore us back to a set point of innate mental health.

Our psychological immune system takes care of our mental well-being just as our physical immune system takes care of our physical well-being. So just as physical pain is designed to let us know when our physical well-being is under threat, our painful, contaminated thinking is designed to send us signals and wake us up when our psychological well-being is under threat. This usually comes in the form of stress, worry, doubt, insecurity, etc. This also lets us know that our Authentic Self is thinking differently.

The problem is that most of us don't respond to the signals from our psychological immune system when it is under threat because we have been conditioned to override it. Our natural, self-correcting psychological immune system that allows us to get out of our painful, contaminated thinking gets overridden by our personal, ego-driven mind.

We are all born with a fully-functioning, self-correcting psychological immune system, but as we grew up, our personal mind was conditioned by the thoughts and habits of others—including our family, our education, our religion, and our culture—about how life works. The more we "buy into" this conditioning, the more it affects our ability to respond to life in a psychologically healthy and natural way.

I am sure you know people who seem to be unusually calm in the face of hardship or crisis, and also people who seem to fall apart at the slightest provocation. People who seem to fall apart at the slightest provocation are convinced that their thoughts are "real." More importantly, that what they are feeling is coming from *outside* of them, from their circumstances, or from other people and they cannot do anything about it. Extreme manifestations of this are people with anxiety and depression.

People who have developed inner resilience allow their psychological immune system to do what it was designed to do. By that I mean when they face hardship, difficulty, and crisis, they intuitively know they can handle anything that comes their way. They step back and with a clear, uncluttered mind, and they allow their self-correcting psychological immune system to take over and heal the situation.

So just as our physical immune system heals our body, our psychological immune system is designed to heal our mind if we allow it to do what it was designed to do. And the healing always comes in the form of new insights, new understanding, new ideas, and new solutions that will enable us to move forward. We just have to trust the system.

Your psychological immune system is part of the inner wisdom of your Authentic Self. However, at some point, you have to start trusting the system.

The way I've come to see it, and I've come to see it this way because I'm constantly putting myself in situations where trusting the inner wisdom of my Authentic Self is all I've got and there's no safety net, every time I trust it, I get more confidence in the fact that it will be there the next time I need it. And at some point, and I am not saying it will come overnight, you will eventually have the same confidence in this inner wisdom that is flowing through your Authentic Self as well.

And the more clearly you start to see that, or at least clear enough to play around with it, the easier it gets to rely on it. And that's the joy of understanding your True Nature and learning how you create and shape your reality moment-to-moment. You develop confidence in the inner wisdom of your Authentic Self, not in your personal, ego-driven mind.

The problem with having confidence in your personal mind is that you will have a lot of confidence when things are going your way. But what happens on those occasions when things turn to crap? Which, I can assure you, they will! When this happens and you've learned to just rely on your personal mind or your ego, you are going to come unraveled. You are going to worry and stress out because you are going to be confused about what to do next.

But if I understand that what I need always comes from the inner wisdom of my expanded Authentic Self, which is my connection with the deeper Intelligence behind life, I can rely on that because it's a universal constant that works every single time if I allow it. It's not dependent on my "situation" or my circumstances. It's always available. It's like gravity. You're not surprised when gravity works. You don't say, "Oh look, we've got gravity today." It's always there.

There is also an element of partnership with the inner wisdom of your Authentic Self. By that I mean that it's always there, but you have to be open to it. When you learn to trust your inner wisdom over your personal, ego-driven mind, you will realize it's always going to be there! You will always get what you need when you need it.

Our Authentic Self never gets discouraged. However, our Ego Self gets discouraged because it doesn't trust the deeper Intelligence behind the system. So, in the beginning, you have to put aside your ego and have "faith" in your Authentic Self that's connected to this deeper Intelligence. But eventually you get to the point where you don't even have to have faith. You just see it in action. In other words, you learn to trust what you *don't see* or what you're *not seeing* in the moment, which are new ideas, new solutions, new possibilities, and new opportunities that are available to you.

If it's about trusting and having confidence in your Ego Self, it becomes about *you,* and then you get caught up in your psychology, but psychology and creativity don't mix. They're totally separate. One is about *thinking,* the other is about *Being,* especially getting out of the way and being in the moment and being in the flow of life.

So, at some point, you have to open up to the fact that you are more than your made-up Ego Self. When something comes from your Authentic Self, it's never about your ego. It's about something bigger than your ego. It's beyond your habitual, contaminated thinking. And if you let that flow through you and guide you, your life will expand beyond anything you can possibly imagine now.

Changing Our World One Thought at a Time

When we live in the misunderstanding of how reality is being created, we don't see that the world we live in individually and collectively is just a reflection of the thinking we have had so far. We talk about the world as this "thing" outside of ourselves. This causes us to ask questions like: "What are we going to do about the education system? What are we going to do about the economy? What are we going to do about racism, terrorism, and domestic violence?"

One of the most interesting things about when people learn how they create their reality moment-to-moment is that they come to realize that we are basically living in a painting of our own creation. And, in doing so, we occasionally have to be reminded that:

Everything we see in the world is a reflection of our individual and collective thinking.

When you think about the problems in the world, I am sure, at least some of the time, you feel very helpless. Sometimes I start to feel overwhelmed because I am tricked by my mind that the problem is "out there" and so is the solution. But the solution to any problem is never "out there."

I live in a city that doesn't change that much, but I change a lot, and so does my experience in the moment. So, I am not seeing the same city every time I drive around. I am seeing my thoughts about the city in the moment. And that changes day to day. Some days it looks like a great place to live and some days it doesn't look so great, but it's neither! It's just being a city until I personalize it. This is how we see the world. The world is the way it is until we personalize it.

People are like this about their children. One moment they are obsessed with them and how wonderful they are and the next moment they want to give them away like puppies. They want to put a sign on them saying, "I am free to live with another family." Everything is about the perception and the meaning we give to it in the moment.

The people in my life, the places in my life, and the things in my world change because my thinking constantly changes. I used to think that my friends, my family, and people in general made me feel different day to day. But the truth is that they're not making me feel anything. Instead, I am experiencing my thinking *about* these people based on my thought-generated perception moment-to-moment.

A simple metaphor for this is that it's like wearing a pair of colored glasses. The color—or the moods and feelings you have about whatever you are looking at—are telling you about the glasses you're wearing, not what you are looking at.

One of the greatest life lessons I have learned is that the world isn't happening *to* me, it's happening *in* me and then I feel the world. So, what's really going on is that I am experiencing my own thoughts about the world, but it looks like "that's the way the world is." We call it "reality," but it's just our thought-generated perception moment-to-moment.

If I don't understand what's happening, I will come from a place of victimization where I believe all the power is "out there" and I am the victim. That means that in order for me to be happy or feel different, I have to change what's "out there." But before we can even begin to change what's "out there," we have to change what's "in here."

Politicians intuitively know this, so they play on our insecurity. Their message is: "Put me in office and I will change what's 'out there,' so that you can have a better life and be happy 'in here.'" We fall for it every single time, and every single time, we end up being disappointed. We keep shooting ourselves in the foot because a permanent solution to any problem will never be "out there."

However, I am not pessimistic. I believe we can change our world regardless of what's happening "out there" or how difficult it looks. A lot of people think that's being naïve, but what's naïve in my mind is thinking that just because the world looks a certain way to us, that's "reality" or "that's the way it is." That's because we don't take into account our capacity for new ideas, new solutions, and new possibilities in any moment.

Miracles happen all the time. However, miracles come from the inside-out, not the outside-in. A miracle is just a new way of looking at something that promotes a new paradigm or new shift in thought. If you think about human progress, it starts with a eureka moment where someone has a new idea or a new thought that changes everything. They are not trying to go backwards and fix what's already there. They are looking for new possibilities and new solutions that we may have never considered before. So, what we call a "miracle" is simply something we have never seen, have never considered before, or don't understand.

At first, the internet was a miracle that looked miraculous to us. But now that we know how it works, we can see it was there all the time. The same thing applies with your mobile phone. When you buy a new mobile phone, you have to connect it to the network. If you didn't know about the existence of the network, it would seem like the ability to use your mobile phone is a miracle, but it was there all the time even before you purchased it.

When you understand how reality is actually created, all of the sudden, you see that the only thing that stands in your way of seeing a different world is how attached you are to your current way of thinking. In many cases, you don't want to let it go. You would rather be "right" than be happy. But if you are willing to look again from a new perspective, it's kind of like a miracle because your experience of reality will change.

The problem is that we spend most of our time and energy trying to fix or change what has already been created instead of creating something new. We have to let go of our old thinking in order to make room for new thinking and new ideas. In terms of resolving the problems that we are facing in the word today, getting people's old thinking out of the way to free up the potential for new thoughts, new ideas, and new solutions is what is going to change the world. Nothing else will work. Nothing!

So, there is no "situation" that cannot be changed or resolved either in our personal lives or in the world. We just don't see how we're going to do it because we're so tricked and so compelled that our current thinking is "right" or something is more unsolvable or intractable than it actually is.

When you look out into the world and see what's happening, it can become a scary thought. We think, "What's the world going to be like based on the way it is now?" And the reason it's a scary thought is because we don't understand that we can reset and start over in any moment. We can let go of what we already think we know and believe and open ourselves up to new thoughts, new possibilities, and new solutions.

And another reason it seems naïve to believe we can change the world is that people have been trying to solve these problems for hundreds or thousands of years without much success. But here's why: the greatest minds in the world have looked at these problems from every possible angle but the most important one—how the world is being created through thought seven and a half billion times every single moment!

We keep trying to solve the problems of war, terrorism, alcoholism, drug abuse, racism, domestic violence, damaging the environment, etc., but those are only *effects*. The reason why we are struggling to solve them is that we are looking at the wrong solution. We are looking at the effects that we have created and then doing our best to try to change the effects. But the cause behind all of these effects will always be the same two things:

1. A misunderstanding of how we individually and collectively are participating in creating our reality moment-to-moment.
2. How we are individually and collectively out of alignment with our Authentic Self and the deeper Intelligence behind life.

These two principles are the cause behind our effects. And until we address them both individually and collectively, we will keep making the same mistakes over and over again because we don't understand how life works as opposed to how we think it works. And when we don't understand how something works, it usually works against us.

So, when you look at all the sadness and horror in the world, what's really going on both individually and collectively is that we keep creating what we don't prefer because we don't understand that every problem we face stems from a misunderstanding of these two principles. This is why I am so passionate about reminding people of their True Nature and how they create their reality moment-to-moment. If we all understood these two principles and how they worked, the world would change immediately.

When we live from our True Nature instead of our personal mind, we can have what we prefer without creating what we don't prefer first. But until we start living from who we are—our Authentic Self—it will be necessary to create darkness in order to find the light because it's much easier to see a candle flame when it's surrounded by darkness. The darkness serves to see the light. The light is what we prefer both individually and collectively. The light allows us to live the most inspired life possible for ourselves and everyone else on the planet.

Individually and collectively, we are stuck where we are because we are caught up in our old thinking. When that happens, nothing will change until we open ourselves up to fresh new thinking—about everything!

You've heard it said, "If we want to change the world, we have to change the way people think." On the surface, that seems like a good idea. It makes sense. There is only one problem with this approach: we have already decided *our* thinking is the "right" thinking. So, when we talk about changing the way people think, what we are really saying is, "How do we get the other people who don't think like us to think the way we do so the world can be the way we want it to be?"

If we believe "we" are right and the "others" are wrong, we compound the problem through a behavioral pattern known as "Otherization." Otherization or Otherizing is a term coined by Dr. Elizabeth Lesser. She describes "Otherization" as the belief that there's "us" and then there are the "others." We are right, and we have the truth. The "others," although well-meaning, are wrong.

This convoluted thinking or "Otherization" eventually turns almost every group, organization, religion, culture, or political system into a system of organized lunacy. "Otherization" has done more to divide, polarize, and separate mankind than anything else. It lies at the root of virtually all of humanity's problems, including war, racism, sexism, homophobia, militant nationalism, and religious self-righteousness.

Neuro-psychological research has demonstrated that as soon as we place people outside of the circle of "us," our brain automatically begins to devalue them and even justifies mistreating them. When you "Otherize" someone or some group, you cannot begin to sense or even know who they really are because your ego has taken over.

The ego wants to be special. This causes us to be attracted to any group, organization, religion, culture, or political system that offers us specialness. In other words, "we" are the "special" ones because we have the truth. The "others" are wrong. They're not "special" like we are. But the problem is that almost every single group, organization, religion, culture, or political system believes their viewpoint is the "right" one.

We can try to change other people's viewpoints through fear, but that's imposing our thinking and beliefs on other people. We are not designed to impose or thoughts and beliefs as an act of will on other people. What we are actually talking about is changing other people's thinking and perception, not as an act of will or forcing them to think and believe what we do, but as an act of *possibility*—that if we all put aside our current beliefs about how we think other people should live, we can create a new and better world together. That's a whole different thing. It opens *all* of us up to see something different, to be wrong about anything or everything, if necessary, in order to make the changes we all desire.

It is not that difficult, but it can be a little uncomfortable at first because we not only have to ask other people to change *their* thinking and beliefs, but we have to be open to changing *our* long-held thinking and beliefs in order for something new to come through for *all* of us. This is the only way we can resolve anything in our personal life or in the world.

Our thinking changes all the time already. It's just being willing to open up in those areas that seem fixed and scary, the areas where we are absolutely sure we're "right," but we are not. When we do that, we take advantage of the natural capacity of the mind for new thoughts and new experiences to come in. And, in doing so, we can help to change the world—one thought at a time.

Chapter 10

THE THEMES
OF OUR LIVES

T here is another perspective on living your magic that I would like to share with you. However, before I do, it's important to understand I cannot "prove" this and it's not my intention for you to either believe it or accept it as the "truth." I'll leave that up to you. This is just my perspective.

My inner knowing has prompted me to understand that there is another dimension to our journey here on this planet of contrasts. By that I mean that each one of us comes here with what we might call a "Theme" for our life. Our Theme includes the time, place, parents, and personal identity we chose for this life. In other words, before emerging from the non-physical into the physical, I set the Theme for my life.

The things that are the greatest challenges in our lives are the Themes that our Soul or Authentic Self chooses to explore in this lifetime. So, there's a Theme for our lives and the destiny our Soul or our Authentic Self wants to experience. But also, there's also free will in terms of *how* we experience it.

You could say the personal Theme or the challenge our Authentic Self or our Soul wants to experience is like a hallway. I use the analogy of a hallway because a hallway is temporary or transient. It's something we go through.

No matter what happens in our life, we WILL walk down that hallway because that is our destiny. But *how* we walk down that hallway is up to us. We can run, we can fly, we can jump, we can go forward, backward, side-to-side, we can be happy, sad, struggle, or whatever we choose. So, the way we experience our journey is not predestined, but we *will* explore that hallway. That is our destiny, but we can explore it any way we want because that's the purpose of free will.

My inner knowing also tells me that there is another level to this that involves something called "Soul agreements" or "Soul contracts." I am just using these definitions because I don't know what else to call them. In other words, there other Souls or Beings that have chosen to participate in our Theme or our experience, and we have chosen to participate in theirs.

Another reason some of us are here is because we have chosen to learn, to teach, to inspire, to manifest, and to help the planet to transform. We knew before we came here that planet Earth is in the process of transforming and, in some way and at some level, we chose to participate and to be part of that.

It's pretty obvious that as a planet we have gone deeply into the darkness. But in all this darkness, whether we realize it or not, we are finding our way to the light. And your mission and mine is to help that light to shine—on everyone!

Again, I am not saying this is the "truth" and you must believe it, but perhaps give it some consideration and see how it resonates within you. I sense a truth behind it and have found it very useful in my understanding of the "bigger picture." I hope you will too!

Pushing Your "Reset" Button

Here's something else you may not be aware of: no matter what is going on in your life, you can push your **reset button** at any time you want. What does that mean? It means that in any moment you can reset and have a new thought that starts from that moment.

You don't have to spend your time trying to fix and change what's already there. You can just reset and start over. When you get out of the way and have less on your mind, your mind automatically resets because your mind is a self-correcting system and its set point is always innate mental health, peace of mind, clarity, optimism, and resilience.

And there's nothing you have to do to reset your system. In fact, any externally-imposed "mind-clearing" techniques, even if they are positive, run the risk of interfering with the natural process of self-correction. As your understanding continues to increase and you learn to live with less on your mind, you free up your self-correcting system to do what it does best, which is to allow you to see things differently.

I am sure you can feel another metaphor coming on so, if you will indulge me, here it is. Imagine there's a can of soup in the kitchen cupboard. Also imagine that you somehow thought that can of soup was a monster. I know this is a silly metaphor but stay with me. You think it's a monster and you wouldn't dare to open the cupboard because you're afraid of it. However, what if, one day, you opened the cupboard door and just looked at it and said, "You know what? I am pretty sure this is just a can of soup."

What happened? The can of soup is still the same. Nothing has changed, but you are no longer seeing it as something it isn't. What changed was your insight and perception about the can of soup. You suddenly see it differently. And there was nothing you had to do to make the change. What really changed your perception was the inner wisdom and Intelligence behind your system coming through. In this case, it was letting you know that it was just a can of soup all along, even though you thought it was a monster!

This built-in, self-clearing, self-correcting mechanism enables us to reset our thinking and perception regardless of the circumstances we are in or what's going on around us or in the world. And we don't have to do anything because having a clear mind, free of contaminated thinking, is our "default setting."

One of the reasons we struggle so much with our thinking is because we think we have to struggle with it. We think it's our job to go in there and sort everything out. And what's been interesting to me as a person who has dozens of degrees and certificates and who has been professionally trained in how to go in there and sort all this stuff out is when I *stopped doing that,* things sorted themselves out much quicker than when I was trying to help the system along. In my desire to help, I was messing up the system because a self-correcting system by its very nature is designed to *fix and correct itself* without any outside help.

It works like a sewage plant that's contaminating a river. If a sewage plant is contaminating a river, the solution is not cleaning the river. The solution is shutting down the sewage plant that's producing the contamination. The moment you shut down the sewage plant, the river will clean itself because the True Nature of the river is that it has a built-in, self-clearing, self-correcting system. If you see what's causing the contamination in the sewage plant, which is a metaphor for our contaminated thinking, you can let it go and it will reset itself. Then everything will start to flow perfectly once again.

The simple truth is that the extent to which we're not living a magical life and experiencing happiness, success, abundance, peace of mind, love, and connection—whether it is in our personal lives or in the world—is directly proportional to the degree which we're not seeing how life actually works. We are out of alignment with reality and we are caught up in an illusion that seems real to us.

All we need to do is step back and allow our mind to reset by getting out of the way and allowing new thoughts, new ideas, and new solutions to show up so we can use them to replace the old, contaminated ones that are not working—the ones we're sure are the truth but are still an illusion.

The idea that we can stop trying to fix and change everything and can take it off our "to-do" list means that no matter how many mistakes we make, we can reset and get back to our "default setting" of innate mental health and clarity as many times as we would like. It's easy, it's natural, and it always gives us a fresh start. In fact, why not just push your reset button every morning and pave the way to a new life, every single day?

It Can't be That Easy!

At this point, there's probably a little voice in your head that's saying, "I would really like to believe this. I want it to be true, but I am still not sure."

Well, here's the thing: you don't have to *believe* it. You just have to *live* it. The results will be self-evident. No proof necessary. How we actually create and shape our reality moment-to-moment is not something we have to believe in. It already works that way. You can check it out yourself.

Now you may also be thinking, "Even if that's true, it can't be that easy." People tend to disagree with simple solutions because we are trained to think that everything is more complicated than it actually is. I have people arguing with me all the time saying, "You make things too simple."

I am used to being criticized by my peers for being too "simplistic" in my approach. Their viewpoint is that life is more complex than my simplisitic approach. If they are right, then everything I've shared with you is pure rubbish.

But what if it is just that simple?

Now, if you want to make changing your life more complicated than it is, I would never want to take away that away from you, but personal change and transformation is not complicated. It's very simple and natural. The problem is that we are so good at looking at what's in our way and making it more complex than it actually is that we don't see that it is that simple. We have this belief: "It took me a long time to get this way so it's going to take a long time to change." However, I don't believe it, nor have I seen any evidence that it is true.

The fastest and easiest route to change is through *insight*. Let's take a look at how easy it is to change once you have a new insight. Let's say you go to work every day the same way. You have been doing it for several years or more. Whatever way you choose to get there, it takes a long time, perhaps forty-five minutes to more than an hour. On top of that, it's not very pleasant and sometimes it can even be stressful.

So, I come along, and I show you a way of getting there in ten minutes. No traffic, beautiful scenery, and a much easier way. Let me ask you this: how difficult do you think it's going to be for you to start taking the new way? It's not difficult at all. You only have to see it and do it **one time** and you are going to start going that new way every single time.

Yet, we think changing our life is hard or it takes a long time. And the longer we have been doing things the old way, the longer it's going to take us to begin doing them the new way. But the truth is: when we see a better way for ourselves, we automatically begin to take it without hesitation, without practice, and without having to remember or study anything.

We take the new way because we genuinely see for ourselves that it's a better way. And this comes from insight, which is another way of saying a "sight from within." That becomes our new reality. And, after that, there's nothing else to do, change, or overcome because we genuinely see there is a better way.

Now let me contrast that with the way we're conditioned to change. We are conditioned to think that change or transformation is not easy. This is especially true if you have had the issue for a long time. Most therapeutic approaches are based on this premise. They are based on taking the *long route* to change which involves looking into your past, discussing your feelings about it, etc.

The problem with that belief system is the therapist or counsellor is going to treat the client or patient *based on their expectation that it takes a long time to change.* This is what allows that idea to perpetuate. While the therapist or counsellor holds on to the argument that change or transformation takes a long time, or that it's not that simple, they also promote reliance on the therapy or therapist. If you buy into that, *it's going to take you a long time to change.* It's not rocket science!

When we don't intuitively understand how we change through insight and we don't understand our True Nature and how we create and shape our reality moment-to-moment, we tend to look for therapeutic approaches, "how-to's," or step-by-step processes to get us from where we are to where we want to be.

This is why the vast majority of personal development books and programs are focused on "how-to" techniques and step-by-step processes. They are designed to change our thinking with *more* thinking or *different* thinking. Unfortunately, as a result, most people have trouble implementing these techniques or strategies, which adds more stress to their life because now they have one more thing on their "to-do" list that they know they "should" be doing but are not doing.

However, when we have an insight into the principles behind how something works, there is nothing to do because these principles inform and guide our thoughts and behaviours in the moment. They allow us to resolve issues that previously seemed impossible as well as resolve and reveal new opportunities that were previously invisible. When we understand our True Nature and how we create our reality moment-to-moment, we can understand anything psychologically or spiritually in our lives and in the lives of others. It's the underpinning of the human experience.

This doesn't mean that once you understand how it works everything is going to be perfect. Everyone has difficulties, hardships, and losses to deal with because life is impersonal. Terrible things are going to happen to all of us individually and collectively. On the other hand, what this means is that you will have a lot more *bandwidth* and *inner resilience* to deal with anything that comes your way and not become overwhelmed by it because you are not all caught up in it. And, in doing so, it won't last long, and you will be on your way once again! Nothing will ever permanently take you down. Every moment can be a new beginning.

Avoiding the "Hope Machine" of Personal Change

Before we end our journey together, I want to reinforce the idea that no matter what is going on in your life, you are not "broken," and you don't need to be "fixed." Hopefully by now you understand that, but in case you snoozed off and missed it, here's a wake-up call.

What it comes down to is this: when we are insecure and don't understand our True Nature and how we create our reality moment-to-moment, we will continue to think that we are not enough, that there is something wrong with us and we need to be "fixed."

And if we buy into that, there are well-meaning, well-intentioned individuals, groups, and organizations standing by, ready to fix us, change us, save us, take away our pain, or make our life better. I call this the "Hope Machine of Personal Change."

Here's how it works. They all operate from the same basic model of:

Problem – Inspiration – Solution

The Problem: We are not good enough the way we are, but we can be better. This is a culturally-accepted belief.

The Inspiration: The inspirational message is that even though we are not good enough the way we are, there is always *hope* that we can be better.

The Solution: The way to get better is to seek the help or advice from an individual, group, organization, or government that will help us to be a better person and live a better life.

We've been "sold" on this model since the day we were born. Here are some examples.

The Beauty Industry

The Problem: Having trouble finding or keeping a man who will love you forever? You need to change the way you look because men are only attracted to beautiful women who look like models and have perfect bodies.

The Inspiration: The good news is that you can look like a model and have a perfect body. It's simple and easy.

The Solution: Buy this anti-aging cream, wear these clothes, alter your body through cosmetic surgery, and men will be attracted to you and love you.

Organized Religion

The Problem: Afraid you won't get to heaven? You should be because God is still upset over the "Apple Incident." And because of it, you are good not enough. You are a sinner. Unless you get "saved," you will be punished, and you won't get into heaven.

The Inspiration: The good news is that thanks to the teachings of Christianity, Judaism, Islam, Hinduism, Mormonism, Jehovah's Witnesses, Seventh Day Adventists, Scientology, and the rest, there is *hope* that you can be saved.

The Solution: Join our religion. Give your life to the teachers, saviors, and prophets behind these religions and you will get a free pass into heaven. Of course, the religion you choose to believe in will always be the "true" one! Aren't we lucky to have found the right one?

The Government

The Problem: Our country is going in the wrong direction. You need a political party that can lead our country, manage your life, know what is best for you, and make decisions for you.

The Inspiration: The good news is that there is always *hope* if you support our polices and hand over your life and your freedom to us.

The Solution: Join our political party. Let us lead the way and decide what is best for you so you don't have to think for yourself. And, if necessary, invade other countries that don't agree with us.

New-Age and Psychic Interventions

The Problem: Not experiencing inner peace and abundance in all areas of your life? It's probably because you have an "energy block" or you are not in touch with your Angel or Spiritual Guide."

The Inspiration: The good news is that if you come in for an astrological, tarot or psychic reading, learn to meditate, tap, chant, or use this special candle or crystal, you can "clear" your energy, find inner peace, and manifest your dreams.

The Solution: Come in for an astrological, tarot or psychic reading, learn to meditate, tap, chant, or use a special candle or crystal (which, by the way, we happen to have in stock), you'll be able to change or attract whatever you want into your life.

Therapy and Life Coaching

The Problem: Not living the life you want? That's because you have limiting beliefs and psychological wounds that are holding you back.

The Inspiration: The good news is that there is always *hope* for you if you use this three-step process, this therapeutic approach, or this success blueprint that will allow you to get rid of your limiting beliefs forever and achieve success and happiness.

The Solution: I am a certified coach, counselor, therapist, NLP trainer, or hypnotist who can help you by using the techniques and processes I have been trained in.

I could go on and on, but you get the idea.

Now before you go out to your garage and get a pitchfork and a torch to burn me at the stake because you may disagree with me, please understand that **I am not against any of these approaches**.

When we don't understand our True Nature and believe we are helpless to resolve our own problems, it makes sense for us to seek access to individuals, organizations, religions, spiritual teachings, personal development techniques, therapeutic approaches, or government interventions to solve our problems or take our pain away. This is the purpose they serve until we wake up to our own True Nature.

All of these approaches can be very *useful*, but from my point of view, they are not *natural* because they all come from the *outside-in*. The way we are designed to transform and live is from the *inside-out* where we learn to trust our *own* internal system, our *own* innate wisdom and deeper intelligence that's guiding us in the right direction every single moment. But we are never going to trust it if we keep looking to others to show us the way.

What I am leading you to is that there is a hidden capacity in human beings to heal themselves, to know what to do moment-to-moment without looking to others to guide us or show us the way. This inner knowing is based on the insight and wisdom that is within each and every one of us. This wisdom will guide us moment-to-moment, taking us beyond our current problem or situation if we trust it and just get out of the way.

Again, I am not knocking these outside-in approaches. They are all well-intentioned. However, notice they also have something in common. They are all about giving us **hope** for the **future**. When will I be able to improve my mental health and well-being? In the future. When will I feel better, be happier, and be more successful? In the future. When will I find salvation? In the future. When will I be able to love my life? You guessed it—in the future.

These futuristic approaches can also become highly addictive because they are based on **hope**. Essentially, we are addicted to hope. Hope, like dope, is a drug because it plays into the illusion that we can or will be happier in the future.

You can experience happiness in the future if you buy this pill, use this product, use these crystals, have your astrological chart read, take this program, read this book, do this therapeutic intervention, hire a coach, use this personal development technique, attend this workshop, become a follower of this religion or spiritual teaching, join this organization, get behind this political party, etc.

When our ego believes that happiness, success, freedom, salvation, love or inner peace are in the future, *we will do or believe in almost anything or anyone to obtain it.*

If we truly want to live our magic, we need to break our addiction to hope and abandon it like the sinking ship that it is. What a beautiful thing it would be to release all attachment to our life being any different than it is right now and just relax into the present moment, surrendering to "what is," knowing that our life and our circumstances will begin to change only as quickly as we stop resisting it and stop judging it.

Instead of living in hope that the future will be better, I have put myself in the mindset that I am living my dream right now. I am no longer striving for tomorrow or for an outcome where I have the illusion that I can be happier. I choose to be happy now! I choose to be my own leader and my own follower by being true to myself and following my highest *joy*, my *excitement*, and my *passion* right now.

When we're in touch with the deeper wisdom of our Authentic Self, we can abandon hope because we can handle anything that comes our way in the moment. And we can reset our mind in any moment because **we are always just one thought away from changing the direction of our life**. We get a fresh start in every moment.

What it boils down to is that we need to stop feeding the "Hope Machine" of personal change with our insecurities. We need to stop selling ourselves and our soul to people who say they can help us change so we can be different from who we are.

What's really happening is that no matter what we do or what we believe, we are all going to feel insecure and doubtful at times. Instead of thinking the answer is outside of you or that you are not good enough the way you are, or that you are psychologically or spiritually broken, just accept the fact that you are human! We are all the same. We suffer, we cry, we feel afraid, we get angry, we fail, we make horrible mistakes, we put ourselves down, and we want to run and hide. Guess what? You're normal! Congratulations!

So, what is to solution to all of this? It is simply **love and self-acceptance.** Love and self-acceptance are the only problems we have ever had in our lives. If we truly want to change our life, the *starting point* of any change is the acceptance of who we are in the moment. It's literally the only acceptable form of personal growth we will ever need.

Your life is exactly the way it is for the moment and as soon as you want it to be different, you will get eaten alive. All that's really happening is that you are caught up in your thinking in the moment, and it will pass if you're willing to let it go.

Remember this important truth:
We can never do any better than the thinking
that looks true to us in any given moment.

Write it down and put it up somewhere where you can remind yourself that this is what's happening in your life in every single moment.

What this means is that you are always doing the best you can based on the thinking that looks real or true to you in any given moment. Your thought-generated perception in the moment is behind everything in your life.

Whatever thought or belief you are holding on to in the moment is what is driving your behavior. But here's the good news: you are never stuck with any thought or belief unless you think it's "real" or "true" and decide to hold on to it. It will always pass if you see it for what it is, which is something you are making up. Every thought and every belief we have is *made up*. We are literally hypnotizing ourselves moment-to-moment.

As you keep having more insight and understanding into your True Nature and how you are creating your reality moment-to-moment, you will wake up from your toxic trances. And when you do, your thinking will change, and your experience will change—but *you* don't need to change.

If you meet a coach, a therapist, a religious, or a spiritual teacher who says you need to change or be different from who you are, consider this: the truth is that you *are*, you *always have been* and *always will be* a capable, interesting, lovable, magnificent, perfect, awe-inspiring miracle of life. And if you just keep reminding yourself of that, that's all you'll ever need.

Where Do You Fit into the Puzzle?

I often have people say to me, "Sometimes I feel like I am not living my highest purpose. There has to be more."

Let me assure you—and of course you don't have to believe me—there is only one thing any of us has to do to fulfil our highest purpose in life and that is to just to **be yourself**. There's nothing else you need to do.

Instead of asking "What is my purpose?" imagine that you are a puzzle piece and life is a giant puzzle board. Your purpose is to fit perfectly on the puzzle board of life so that you live in synchronicity. This allows you to attract the perfect friends, opportunities, relationships, and everything else you desire.

Like a picture puzzle, there are thousands of pieces that fit together, but none of the pieces are better or more significant than the others. Each one is uniquely shaped. Each one is different. Whatever shape your piece is, that's the shape you need to be, because if you try to be the shape you're not, you won't fit in with the other pieces and you cannot create the whole picture of All That Is.

There has never been another you, there is no other you now, and there will never be another you in the future. Obviously, "All That Is" felt that it was necessary to have you as part of All That Is. It would be incomplete without you. And in just creating you, the unique Spirit, the unique signature vibration that you are, just being yourself is the greatest gift you can give back to All That Is.

You do this by just believing in yourself and doing what comes naturally to you to the best of your ability in any given moment. And if you follow your highest *joy*, your *passion*, your *excitement*, and your *creativity* to the best of your ability in any given moment, you will be fulfilling your highest purpose. You will be living your magic.

And if at times you don't feel like you're doing your best, that's okay too. You're just caught up in your thinking in the moment and it will pass if you are willing to let it go. And once you reset, you're back to doing your best, so you've fulfilled your highest purpose once again!

Everyone has the same purpose: just to be yourself! That's all you need to do. *How* you do it, the *way* you do it, and what path you take is not *part* of your purpose. They are an *expression* of your purpose. But if you will simply be the unique shape or piece of the puzzle that you are, it will fit automatically and harmoniously with all the other pieces who are also willing to be who they are. And when you fit them all together, they make up the whole picture which then supports all the other pieces.

What happens sometimes is that your puzzle piece tends to get bent out of shape when you are not living from your Authentic Higher Self. Let's say you are someone who tries to please others, or you devalue yourself because you think you are not good enough. Let's say you are not completely being yourself. You are more guarded instead of being open and vulnerable or you tend to take everything too seriously. That's being unauthentic. Your Ego Self has taken over and you are caught up in your contaminated thinking.

When that happens, your puzzle piece gets bent out of shape or out of alignment. But when you have less on your mind and you are not caught up in your contaminated thinking, your **original puzzle piece** automatically resets and goes back into alignment with this deeper Intelligence behind life.

As you go back to the true shape of your original puzzle piece, you may also notice that the people in your life—your friends, your work, and even the relationships that you are connected to—may no longer feel right. They may start to drain you. And as they begin to drain you, the next important step is to *let go*. To let go of the people, the things, and the ideas that are no longer serving you. They have served their purpose for a time, but by gently letting them go with love and appreciation, you open up to new possibilities, new ideas, and new people coming into your life. It is always about going back to being youself, to being your natural piece of the puzzle, and simply letting go and allowing synchronicity to bring the rest of the pieces of the puzzle together.

However, I need to remind you that when you are living through your Authentic Self, you will be travelling to the beat of a different drummer. Some people will think you are crazy or naïve for even considering living this way.

There is a saying that goes like this: "Those who dance are thought to be insane by those who cannot hear the music."

Trust me, there is a good chance that other people will not hear your music, but that's okay. It's not about, "I need to get everyone to dance to this music." It's about you dancing to your *own* music. And there is no required way to dance. If you dance to your own music, your way of changing yourself and the world around you will unfold beautifully inside you and that will be mirrored in your physical reality.

When you start to hear the music, when you start to follow what comes up from the deeper wisdom and Intelligence of your Authentic Self, things will unfold as if by design. You will find yourself running into the right people and the right situations at the right time. And if you are open to it, it's a heck of a ride!

You Have Access to Superpowers!

When you live through the deevper Intelligence of your Authentic Self and not your ego, you have access to superpowers!

You don't have to be like Clark Kent and put on a costume, a cape, and a mask to step into your superpowers. Whether Superman (or Superwoman) is dressed in their normal everyday clothes or not, *they still have their superpowers*, but if they don't know it or believe it, they will think they have to put on the costume, the cape, and mask and be *someone else* in order to access their superpowers.

Kryptonite is the only thing that can weaken their superpowers. Kryptonite is a metaphor for Superman or Superwoman *not believing in themselves*. Our Kryptonite is our own limited thinking and believing that we have to be someone else in order to access our superpowers and live our magic.

So, here's the question you must answer: is *Living Your Magic* and being true to yourself possible or impossible for you? The great boxer Muhammad Ali once said: "Impossible is just a big word thrown around by small people who find it easier to live in the world they've been given rather than to explore the power they have to change it. Impossible is not a fact. It's an opinion."

If you look at the word "impossible," to most people, it means something is not possible. However, there is also another way to look at the same word which is to change it to "I'm Possible." It's the same spelling, but a different meaning. So, every time you see the word "impossible," think, "I'm possible," and remind yourself: "I am a Master of Possibility. Anything is possible if I choose to accept it is possible."

Most people are living in a constructed reality where they are trying hard to be a good person and to do what others want them to do. They want to be "normal." They are trying to fit in so they can be accepted and validated by other people. It's even worse now due to social media because no matter what you do or say, someone has an opinion.

When something is "normal," it is mid-range. Normal is living in the center of the bell curve, which means there is half above and half below. The problem with being "normal" is that as a society, we have set the bar really low in terms of what normal means for our lives. Yet, people cling to the idea that they want to be normal and fit in and be like everybody else.

Instead of being normal, you should strive to be **exceptional**. In other words, if you fit in and you are like other people, you are living a life that is well below the bell curve. In order to live your magic, you have to choose to live an exceptional life and give up being "normal." That's what *exceptional* means. You cannot be *exceptional* without being the *exception*.

We have to learn to trust ourselves. To trust that "inner knowing" part of us which we have been calling our Authentic Self. We always have access to this inner creative wisdom and deeper Intelligence that guides us moment-by-moment. When we trust this wisdom instead of living out of the suitcase of our old ideas and theories about how life works, our challenges don't seem so challenging and our problems seem to dissolve before we need to solve them. Inspired ideas and insights are our constant companions and we regain our full power to live the most magical life possible.

A New Beginning

L et's go back to *The Wizard of Oz*. Near the end of the story, Glinda, the good witch, reveals that Dorothy has always had the power to get home, but she would've never believed it if she had been told that in the beginning. **She had to discover it for herself.**

Dorothy discovers that she has all the power she needs within her. When she taps her ruby red slippers together and repeats the phrase "there's no place like home," she wakes up in her bed, surrounded by her family. Dorothy doesn't believe them at first when they tell her that her adventure in Oz was a dream. She protests that it was a real place, but they reassure her that she never left home, that it was just a dream.

When she finally realized it was a dream and was asked what she had learned, Dorothy says, "If I ever go looking for my heart's desire again, I won't look any further than my backyard, because if it isn't there, I never really lost it to begin with." In other words, whatever she desired was within her, not "out there."

You have everything within you right now to start living your magic. As you keep gaining more insight and understanding into your True Nature and how you create and shape your reality moment-to-moment, you will start to live in a friendlier world. You will insightfully understand that you don't need to change other people or anything else "out there" to feel better "in here." You start to see, "Oh, it's just my thinking. I'm making that up" and you just let it go of it. And when you do, you're ready for a new thought, a new opportunity, a new solution, and a new possibility.

Imagine a life where worrying about the future is a thing of the past and you are able to quickly find your way back home to the peace and clarity of your True Nature. Whether you realize it or not, that is already happening inside of you right now and it is coming from a better place than you were operating from five years ago, one year ago, three months ago, or even a few moments ago.

The reason I know this is because the world is going to look different to you from now on. You will see things more clearly and more deeply. And while you may not be aware of it yet, your understanding right now is deeper than most of humanity.

Here is something else to consider. Regardless of where your life is right now, you should celebrate how far you have come and how well you are doing given the fact that *you will never know this little again!*

It's based on the truth that when you see more, you will know more. And it's inevitable that if you keep looking within, trusting yourself, and taking inspired action, you will continue to see more.

So, if you can do this well with the understanding that you currently have, it seems self-evident that as you increase your understanding of how life works, you're going to do even better! And when you are doing better within yourself, you can live your magic, enjoy your mind, and enjoy your life.

Just be patient with yourself. Even a small increase in your understanding of your True Nature and how you create your reality moment-to-moment can have a huge impact on the quality of your life. Remember, life is like a magic trick: once you know how the trick works, you can never be fooled by it again. Now that you know how the magic trick of life works, you will never get fooled by it again!

I hope you've enjoyed your journey with me and that you have gained some fresh new insights and understandings that will help you to stay true to yourself and live your magic. The very fact that you have come this far indicates that at some level you know you are "this close" to letting go of all the stuff in your life that doesn't serve you. I am grateful that you have chosen me to punt you over the edge! Thank you for allowing me to do that!

Regardless of where you are right now, you can begin again because you get a fresh start in every moment. It's about who you choose to be in this moment. And whoever you choose to be in this moment has nothing to do with who you were in the past or who you will be in the future because there's only this moment. That's why they call it the "present" moment—because it's a gift!

Start right now in this moment to act on your **passion**, your **joy**, your **creativity,** and your **excitement**. Everything you want to be, you already are. You are simply on the path to discovering it. This is how you can "live your magic" effortlessly while staying true to yourself.

ACKNOWLEDGEMENTS

I would like to take a moment to acknowledge Michael Neil, Jamie Smart, and James Tripp for the massive influence they have had on my life and my work. I also want to acknowledge my best friend Ian for always being there for me. You helped more than you can imagine. And finally to my publisher, Morgan James, who has supported my work over the years and has allowed me to share this work with you.

ABOUT THE AUTHOR

Dr. Robert Anthony is a Mind Magician and Personal Change Strategist with over 30 years' experience in almost every aspect of mind power development. This includes a PhD and extensive training and certifications in almost every aspect of psychology and self-development including NLP, EFT, and Hypnosis.

He is originally from the USA but has lived in Australia for the past 18 years. His two best-selling books, *Beyond Positive Thinking* and the *Ultimate Secrets of Total Self Confidence*, have sold over 2 million copies worldwide. He was also acknowledged by Rhonda Burns in the introduction to her book as an inspiration behind "The Secret."

As a Personal Change Strategist, he worked his "magic" with individuals from all walks of life including entrepreneurs, personal development trainers, hypnotists, couples, students, authors, dancers, actors, singers, and a few well-known Hollywood celebrities to help them to create powerful changes in their lives.

As a Mind Magician, he also raises money for charitable organizations with his popular "Mind Tapped" show where he uses his background hypnosis, psychology, body language, suggestion, magic, and the mystic arts to take his audience on an entertaining journey into the power of their mind.

Printed in the USA
CPSIA information can be obtained
at www.ICGtesting.com
JSHW082206140824
68134JS00014B/458

9 781642 795073